how to be *french*

how to be *french*

Margaret Ambrose

NEW
HOLLAND

First published in Australia in 2005 by
New Holland Publishers (Australia) Pty Ltd
Sydney • Auckland • London • Cape Town

14 Aquatic Drive Frenchs Forest NSW 2086 Australia
218 Lake Road Northcote Auckland New Zealand
86 Edgware Road London W2 2EA United Kingdom
80 McKenzie Street Cape Town 8001 South Africa

National Library of Australia Cataloguing-in-Publication Data:

    Ambrose, Margaret, 1969- .
    How to be French.

    ISBN 1 74110 244 8.

    1. Ambrose, Margaret, 1969- - Journeys - France. 2. Women
    journalists - Victoria - Melbourne - Biography. 3. France -
    Description and travel. I. Title.

    070.484092

Publisher: Fiona Schultz
Managing Editor: Angela Handley
Project Editor: Liz Hardy
Designer: Joanne Buckley
Production: Kellie Matterson
Printed in Australia by Griffin Press, Adelaide

10 9 8 7 6 5 4 3 2 1

Cover photo: Photolibrary.

Acknowledgments

There are many people who made this book possible, but special thanks go to my mother, Shirley Caulfield, and my partner in life and best friend, Lincoln Hepburn, for their encouragement and unwavering belief in me.

Thanks also to my siblings, Geoff, Lisa, Rich and Liz, and my best friends Carol and Kieran for their love, and to the beautiful Ruffy, who forfeited many walks so this book could be written.

A huge thanks to all the staff and students at the Alliance Française de Melbourne, who made learning French so much fun and so memorable, especially my dear friends Douglas and Jean-Philippe. Also Alison, my best friend in Paris.

And finally, a big thanks to the kind and wonderful Julie, who is still the only person I know who wants to be French as much as me.

About the author

Margaret Ambrose is editor of the Australian women's online magazine, theLounge.com.au and works as a freelance journalist in France, Australia and the United States. In 1999, Margaret enrolled in her first French class at the Alliance Française de Melbourne. After five years of study she believes it was a decision that not only led to her learning a language, but changed her life. Margaret lives in Elwood, Victoria, with her partner and an assortment of French language books, movies and CDs. She regularly travels to Paris, where she is a contributing journalist with a number of French magazines.

Contents

Part Three: Advanced

Part One:
Beginners

Chapter 1
Margie's first French class

Initial contacts

Habiter (to live)	*Vous habitez où?*
	J'habite à Elwood.
Être (to be)	*Êtes-vous mariée?*
	Je suis célibataire.
Avoir (to have)	*Vous avez quel âge?*
	J'ai 32 ans.

Sophie was a bohemian. Looking at her, we could tell straightaway that she spent her days drinking coffee, reading left-wing, underground newspapers and screaming at her husband in public. She carried her head high with pride, a water bottle under her arm and had a mouth that was shaped in a pout. Sophie would sit on the steps of the Alliance, sucking in the last drags of a cigarette with an expression that said, 'fuck off, you fool'. She was everything we imagined a French teacher to be.

There is no bohemian equivalent in Australia; we have no group that is collectively called 'the intellectuals'. Our socially conscious tend to be the grunge or hippie, uni student type, not the designer shoes wearing type. In a way that's not often achieved by women outside Europe, Sophie managed to combine smart with sexy.

Just stepping through the doors of the Alliance Française language school made Freda and I feel French. The Alliance is on one of the most exclusive streets in Melbourne's fashionable St Kilda in a transformed residential house. The interior is well maintained and the parquetry floor is polished to a high sheen. Reproductions of French masterpieces hang on the walls beside framed posters of classic French movies.

The classrooms have retained their original features, including fireplaces, and the bookshelves house leather-bound copies of French classics. Although the Alliance is quiet and has a serious and studious feel, it is also welcoming.

As well as the obligatory French lessons of early high school, I had actually attended a couple of semesters at the Alliance, on and off, over the years. These attempts generally occurred immediately after a trip to Europe, while I was still high on European culture and imagined that if I could speak French I would somehow be more French, and less the Aussie girl who had spent a couple of weeks in Paris. But I had never stuck it out longer than the one semester.

I was too busy at work, I said. It was too hard to get there. I had a very active social life. All of these excuses were true, but it is also true that if you are committed to something, you make the time—and two hours a week isn't a huge sacrifice.

I enjoyed studying and the process of learning another language, but I was, frankly, terrified every time I walked into the classroom. It was always the same. After you get through the basics of grammar and vocabulary, the classroom becomes an out of control environment. Not that the teacher suddenly loses control of the students or the class would disintegrate into a pack of wild beasts. It was simply a huge jump from reciting verb conjugations and basic expressions to actually having to answer questions (that you could barely understand) by formulating on-the-spot sentences in front of a class full of strangers. Even if you were lucky enough to understand the question being asked, your response almost always made you sound like an idiot.

Sitting there waiting for the humiliation terrified me. But this time had the potential to be different. Freda was going to be with me, and just knowing I had a friend by my side gave me added security. When I walking into the Alliance that night, it was the first time I actually felt excitement and not dread.

Freda and I were a few minutes late for our first lesson, and when we entered the classroom we were faced with about ten very nervous faces, and Sophie.

'*Bonjour*', said Sophie with a smile as she motioned to us that we sit down. '*Je m'appelle Sophie.*'

Freda looked at her with a blank expression, but I had attended enough French classes to know how I was expected to respond. '*Bonjour. Je m'appelle Margaret.*'

I quickly realised that most people in the class had not one word of French, and that Sophie had every intention of not speaking one word of English. This was clearly freaking out most of the class.

'*Quelle est votre profession?*' she asked the middle-aged man who was closest to her. He had been fidgeting since we arrived and was beginning to sweat profusely. Sweaty Guy laughed nervously and quickly scanned the room to see if anyone else looked as though they understood what she had said. '*Pardon?*' he stammered in his best French accent.

'*Votre profession?*' Sophie said very clearly, '*Je suis lectrice*'. She pointed to herself. '*Et vous êtes … ?*'

Still no response, so Sophie moved onto the next person, a younger looking professional who had managed to get the gist of the question. '*Je suis* … a lawyer?' she asked.

'*Avocate*', responded Sophie, smiling.

'*Je suis avocate*', responded the woman.

'*Bravo!*' said Sophie. I was next. '*Quelle est votre profession?*'

'*Je suis journaliste*', I said proudly and confidently. Sophie clapped her hands in glee and moved on to the next person, who by now understood the question.

Understanding the question, of course, didn't mean you knew how to answer. Freda, who had no experience with French, had caught on that saying '*Je suis*' meant something like 'I am', although she didn't understand that *je* was I and that *suis* was a form of the verb *être*, to be. To her, it was just making the sound of 'jeswee'.

Plus, some professions were easier to describe than others. *Journaliste, médecin, lectrice* were all pretty straightforward. But when it came to Freda's turn, she had to say, 'Jeswee a human resources and administration manager for an organisation that produces exercise equipment'.

Part One: Beginners

Once we had got through our professions, we moved on to where we lived, how old we were and whether we were married and had children.

I had sworn to myself that this time I was going to stick with French classes. I was determined that this time was going to be different; this time I was not going to be defeated and give up; this time I was going to be prepared. And knowing already that the first few classes would be all about introductions, I had done the preparation.

'I am 32 years old', I answered, when instructed to tell the rest of the class about myself. 'I live in Elwood with my boyfriend and my dog, Ruffy. I am a journalist and I write articles about health and beauty. I like reading, watching films and going to the beach.'

Okay, in English it doesn't sound particularly mind-blowing, but this was the first class of Beginners 1, and I had spent two hours the night before working on this little speech. It wasn't just a case of looking words up in the dictionary—once I knew the words I had to put them into actual sentences. And if I could only get that nervous quiver out of my voice …

Sophie raised her eyebrows, clearly impressed. This is good, I thought. 'I would like to learn French because my sister speaks French. She lives in Québec and she studies translation at the university. I hope that I can talk with her in French.'

I breezed through the class, because I knew all of it already and was able to answer the questions with at least a little bit of confidence, although my accent, I knew, was shocking.

Freda, to her credit, was trying very hard and had her face creased in concentration for the entire two hours. When the class was over Freda broke into a smile and started talking to me enthusiastically. I could tell she had struggled, but she had also been challenged and was as a result invigorated.

As traumatic as the first class was for the students, Sophie was empathetic. She had a small voice, a small laugh and long eyelashes that she batted a lot. She was sweet and relaxed in the classroom, and while she took learning a language very seriously, she never stressed the students. Often she would burst out laughing at a student's attempt to roll their r's or pronounce a word of more than two syllables, which saved a few tears. Secretly, I wasn't sure if she was laughing with us or at the thought of the reaction of her bohemian friends when she retold the story over a bottle of red that evening.

Which is exactly how Freda and I liked to define ourselves. Privately, we believed that was how we should be living—spending afternoons in groovy cafes, discussing society and art, with our fabulously clever friends. Living less the life of suburban office workers, and more the life of bohemians and artists. It was one of the driving forces of us deciding to learn French at the Alliance Française de Melbourne. That, and the fact that we had already booked our tickets to Paris.

The idea for spending the Millennium Eve in Paris was born on New Year's Eve in Dublin the year before. In 1999, my immediate family gathered together for Christmas at Mum's house in Ireland. On New Year's Day the papers were full of the usual wrap-up of celebrations around the world, but also with previews of how each city planned to celebrate the Millennium the following year. There was nothing really special about Paris except, apparently, there were going to be fireworks from the Eiffel Tower, but I knew I would be there.

I don't recall ever thinking too much about the important details. I didn't know anyone living in Paris and I didn't know anyone who was planning to go to Paris. I just knew I was going to go.

Over the years I had been to Paris several times, usually as part of a whirlwind backpacking adventure or as a stopover on the way to visit Mum in Ireland. Of course, like everyone else, I had been subjected to the 'most romantic city in the world' ideal of Paris, and on every visit I marvelled at its physical beauty.

Yet, to me Paris was more than a gorgeous city with a romantic aura— it was a place where dreams become reality. At home in Melbourne, I was surrounded by people who watched what food they put into their body, recycled rubbish religiously and even had things called 'clothing allowances' they put in something called a 'budget'.

In a world that was becoming increasingly sensible, to me, Paris was the ultimate fairytale. Paris was a place where beauty, elegance and style reigned supreme; where every girl could be a princess, surrounding herself in beauty and adoring males. She wasn't expected to have a stance on global warming, or pretend to be concerned with the growing development in her suburb. On a magical night like Millennium Eve, it was the only place to be.

When I returned from Ireland, I told Freda of my plans. Despite my dreams of fairytales, my reality was, well, all too real. Freda and I both worked for a company that manufactured home gym equipment, which was situated on an industrial estate in the outer suburbs of Melbourne. Freda was in middle management. I worked in the publications department as editor and chief writer for the health and wellbeing magazine that Moonlite produced, which also promoted their products.

Freda was someone who was super-organised and super-focused. She knew what she was doing and why. Everything about her was structured and perfect, from her suits to her home ownership plans. Freda was the last person on Earth you would call spontaneous.

One day at work, I was sitting in Freda's very tidy office telling her about New Year's Eve in Dublin and my plans for Paris. 'How much do you think the airfare will be?' she asked.

'About $1700,' I said, 'but if I start saving money now I'll be able to do it'.

'And how much is the hotel?'

'About 70 francs a night', I replied. 'It's not a flash hotel, but it is really central and …'

'Okay, I'm coming with you.'

'What?' It was so unexpected.

'I'm coming with you,' Freda smiled. 'I've never been to Paris!'

By the end of the week, Freda had drawn up a budget and saving schedule and had begun collecting quotes from different travel agents. In her office there was an arch-lever file with the beginnings of all the information for our trip.

I could understand Freda's attraction to Paris, because it was the same romantic mystique that also lured me. Freda loved glamour: clothes, make-up and cosmetics. I think she imagined she had quite an affinity with French women. She was assertive and confident, yet unashamedly feminine. The timing was right for her, too. She had just completed her second degree, which she was doing part-time, and had closed the door on a semi-relationship with a man who wouldn't commit and didn't even seem to know what he wanted from one day to the next.

Having someone to share the fantasy with made the anticipation of our trip that much more exciting. We began by collecting magazine articles and pictures of Paris. Freda and I would huddle together in our offices and gush over the beauty of Paris and the knowledge that we were going to be there on such a momentous occasion. Our excitement about our trip was fuelled by the little dose of France we got at the Alliance.

The next few lessons continued the theme of first introductions, which wasn't as simple as knowing how to add different endings to the phrase, *'Je suis …'* We had to know how to ask people about themselves and that involved using *'tu'*, or *'vous'* if you wished to be formal, instead of *'je'*, and every time we changed the subject, the verb also had to be changed.

Although I had a little more understanding than most of the class, we were all in the same boat. We understood about one per cent of what Sophie would say and that was largely because of the hand movements or sound effects that accompanied her statements or questions. After a few classes, though, everyone understood the importance of seating arrangements.

The tables were arranged in a U-shape with the teacher's table at the front, facing us. Sweaty Guy, who had seated himself at the first table on the left, soon regretted his decision, which was made in panic in the first class, when he had a strong desire to seat himself and blend in as soon as possible. Sweaty Guy was the first person called on every time Sophie asked a question. She would then move clockwise around the class. By the time she got to Freda and I, we not only understood the gist of the question, we had been able to formulate a response.

If Sweaty Guy had any thoughts of changing his seat, he would have soon realised it was futile. In French class, the seat you choose in the first class is the one you are expected to sit in for the rest of the semester. It was an unwritten rule and one created by the students. I think it comes from the fact that in foreign language classes you are so out of your depth and so ignorant of everything going on around you, you cling to the smallest bit of security you can. And if that means a regular seat, so be it.

Chapter 2
An evening with Xamuel, the frightening substitute teacher

Verbs: the present tense

Faire (to do, make): *je fais* (I do) *nous faisons* (we do)

tu fais (you do) *vous faites* (you do)

il/elle fait (he does) *ils font* (they do)

Aimer (to like/love): *j'aime* (I like) *nous aimons* (we like)

tu aimes (you like) *vous aimez* (you like)

il aime (he likes) *ils aiment* (they like)

The class was sitting patiently and silently (well, for the most part—Sweaty Guy was nervously tapping his pencil on his desk), although Sophie was already ten minutes late. We were all flipping through our books revising what we learnt in the last class and nervously looking at what this class had in store. Suddenly the door burst open with a crash as it hit the wall, and in barrelled Gerard Depardieu, announcing in a enormously booming voice, *'Je m'appelle Xamuel!'*

He stood there for a few moments as if allowing us the time to soak up the importance of what he had said. Then he slammed the door shut and began booming some sort of introduction, although it was so rapid I am convinced nobody in the class understood a word. He spoke at a level five times the normal volume and paced across the room, violently gesticulating. Books didn't exactly rattle on the shelves, but it seemed like they were about to.

The only peace in the entire lesson was directly after Xamuel said something he believed to be deeply profound, and he would stare into space like Napoleon contemplating his achievements. Then he would start yelling all over again.

'There is never another letter following the letter *x*', he exclaimed dramatically to a student who had made what seemed to be the ultimate faux pas, by trying to spell the word *ecchymose* (bruise) and mistakenly replacing the cch with an x. 'Except after my name.' Dramatic silence. '*Xamuel!*' Then silence. I think he was expecting a round of applause. He revered the French language and spoke of it like it was his lover. When someone asked him a question about an irregular verb, he stared dreamily into space. 'Ah, that is the mystery of the French language ...'

Xamuel was flamboyant in a way that did French stereotypes proud. He was short and plump and had abominable dress sense. He wore an old baggy jumper covered in lint balls, checked baggy cotton pants with patterned socks and brogues.

Thankfully, we spent the class correcting the homework from the week before. That meant that at least we had some idea of what we were supposed to be doing. Xamuel ordered us to open our books at page 'blah blah blah'. In a show of unity, the person sitting closest to Xamuel saw what page he had opened the book to, and the message was relayed in whispers to the back of the room.

Xamuel handed a texta to Sweaty Guy and ordered him to write the answer to the first question on the whiteboard. They were all exercises in *la négation*. We had been given simple sentences, which we were supposed to turn into the negative. The first sentence was *J'aime le sport.* Sweaty Guy wrote with a wobbly hand, *Je ne aime pas le sport.*

'*Non, non, non, non, non!*' bellowed Xamuel. 'Blah blah blah blah blah!' Sweaty Guy stood at the board, frozen, not having understood a word that Xamuel said. It was only when Xamuel rubbed out the *ne aime* and replaced it with *n'aime* that he understood his mistake—if the verb begins with a vowel, you always use *n'* instead of *ne*.

Xamuel handed the texta to the next student, who didn't look quite as nervous as the first. Exercise two read *Il est sympathique*. He wrote on the board, *Il n'est pas sympathique.*

'*Bravo!*' yelled Xamuel, and the man returned to his seat triumphant.

It was my turn next but I was confident, if only for the reason that I had already corrected my answers from the back of the book. The third statement was, *Il mange beaucoup*.

I wrote on the board, *Il ne mange pas beaucoup*.

'*Magnifique!*' exclaimed Xamuel, clasping his hands together in delight. '*C'est parfait!*'

I smiled sweetly and went to hand the texta to the next student. '*Non!*' demanded Xamuel. '*Continue!*' Not sure exactly why, I looked at the next statement and wrote the corresponding answer on the board, which of course was correct. Xamuel was in raptures. Then he made me answer the next question. And the next and the next.

I was having a ball. I was the centre of attention and Xamuel matched every answer I got correct with a new whoop of praise. By the end of the class, I had been at the board for forty-five minutes and no-one in the rest of the class had to answer a question, which I am sure they were secretly pleased about.

At the end of the class, Xamuel gathered his things and left in the same whirlwind of commotion with which he had entered the room. 'I think he really liked me!' I exclaimed to Freda. She rolled her eyes. 'Margie,' she said, 'he just spent the whole class checking out your arse'. The people next to us nodded solemnly in agreement.

★★★★

'I've got what I need so I'm happy.' That was Freda's explanation as to why she wouldn't be continuing French into semester two. Freda now had enough French to go shopping and eat in Paris. Yet the truth was, Freda didn't really enjoy learning French. It didn't suit her personality.

Freda was in control of every aspect of her life. She was a very well-respected professional, a home owner, and was admired by her family and friends. Regular humiliation didn't feature in her life. It didn't take long for us to realise that when you study another language, humiliation is part of the deal. Freda suddenly found herself in a situation where, not only wasn't she the most knowledgeable person in the room, but for a large part of the time she didn't understand what was going on or what to say when prompted. She didn't enjoy laughing at herself and she certainly didn't enjoy people laughing at her. Going to France was fun, but learning French wasn't. It was hard work that required dedication and it didn't interest Freda.

I was nervous about continuing French without a friend; being without Freda would mean I was absolutely on my own. When we were together we could help each other with our homework and explain things that the other person may not have understood. Admittedly, it was normally me who was doing the explaining, but it was good to know Freda was there. Especially in class. When worst came to worst and one of us seriously did not have a clue what Sophie expected us to say, the other could be relied on to whisper under her breath in English.

I decided to enrol in Beginners 2 for a couple of reasons, the strongest being that I feared I was slipping into mediocrity. When I was studying journalism and editing I had imagined what it would be like to work on a fast-paced publication in a vibrant environment and come home from work with my heart racing. I imagined working with people who were creative and inspiring. A warehouse in outer suburban Melbourne was not where I saw myself, and people who stood around the photocopier complaining about the arrangements for the office Christmas party were not the colleagues I imagined.

I saw being monolingual as terribly unsophisticated. On previous trips to Europe I met people who almost always spoke English, as well as their native tongue, and then varying degrees of a third language. They were able to travel from country to country, speaking the language as if they were home. To me, having only one language furthered my sense of mediocrity.

Of course, many people travel the world with only English and there was nothing stopping me exploring the world as one of them. But these people were just tourists. I wanted to be at home in Europe. I didn't want to be a spectator of a glamorous and exciting life; I wanted to be a participant.

Studying at the Alliance also meant that for two hours every week I would totally forget work and my fears of slipping into suburbia. I was unhappy at Moonlite mainly because my journalistic and writing needs weren't being stimulated. Filing health and fitness stories did interest me, but for the most part I was simply writing copy that supported the products Moonlite imported. I was working with people who didn't know anything about publishing and rarely thought about the publications the company produced, unless there was an error that they could gleefully point out.

It was the culture of the place that really got me down. Moonlite had a very oppressive culture. There were a few women in key positions who seemed to be ruled solely by their own misery and the desire to destroy the happiness of others in the office. The manager of accounts would regularly watch the sign in/sign out book to make sure that the time that people returned from lunch matched the time they put in the book—to the minute. She was in cohorts with the CEOs personal assistant and together they were responsible for creating a prison-like environment.

My supervisor was drawn into these petty power struggles, not because she was mean or miserable, but because she was insecure. Edith was officially head of the marketing department. She had a great sense of humour and was fun to work with, but she came with her own set of problems. All Edith wanted from life was for everyone to love her. If she thought that the CEO was unhappy with the department, she would work herself into such a state that she actually got chest pains. Edith would always stick up her hand if there was any extra work that needed to be done and, to my annoyance, she often volunteered for me to do extra work to make the CEO happy. Sometimes I complained, but not often, because Edith was essentially sweet and I genuinely felt sorry for her.

Freda did too. Technically, Freda had nothing to do with my department. I consulted her when I needed to ask something about what was lawful to say in an article, and she also proofread articles, but she was her own department. And yet, Edith would be in Freda's office several times a day, double-checking everything so she wouldn't 'make a mistake and get into trouble'. Plus, she simply had no faith in her own abilities to make decisions.

Only once did Freda react. Edith had been on annual leave for a week and during that week Freda and I had lunch together every day. On her return, the head of accounts, in conjunction with the PA, told Edith that Freda and I had spent every minute of the day in each other's offices gossiping about other staff and causing trouble.

Edith believed me when I told her that this wasn't true and she could see that all my work had been done. That wasn't what concerned her. She was worried because her department had pissed the two bullies off. So she told me I wasn't allowed to be friends with Freda anymore.

I was shocked and protested that I could be friends with whomever the hell I wanted and that the others could forget it. Edith agreed, but begged me not to cause trouble. I told Freda, who was furious. In true Freda fashion, she didn't try talking to the two troublemakers. She went straight to the CEO and made a complaint. He spoke to the two women concerned and we were allowed to be friends again.

That was the oppressive schoolyard mentality of Moonlite. The environment of fear only added to Edith's insecurities, and she became more and more anxious. She had tried to talk me out of going to Ireland with my family because it meant that I would be out of the office for four weeks. I insisted, and, as I suspected, the publications department didn't fall apart. But mainly because Freda took on the role of backstop. Now, though, we were both going to be away at the same time and we just knew that Edith would sabotage our plans. We thought about what we were going to do and came up with a strategy.

First of all I put in the form for my holidays. After some grumbling about the lifestyles of the rich and famous, Edith (who also resented anyone who actually enjoyed their lives) signed my leave form. Freda didn't let on that she was planning to go with me. About a week later, Freda approached her own supervisor, the CEO, with her holiday request, which he signed. Freda waited until she knew Edith was in my office to burst in and say excitedly, 'Guess what? I got my holiday approved! I'm going to Paris with you!'

'What?' I exclaimed with mock surprise. 'That's fantastic!'

Edith's face fell but she had no option but to act happy for us. Anyway, there was nothing she could do.

At the time, Freda was possibly my best friend. She was certainly the person I felt was most like me. Despite the drudgery of our work, Freda and I both maintained visions of glamour. We both considered ourselves to be intelligent and attractive, and liked to tell ourselves we had the world at our feet. In our minds, the impending trip to Paris for the Millennium Eve was indicative of this. So was learning French.

One lunchtime, Freda and I went shopping. We walked through the scarf and hat section of the local Myer department store and I decided to try on some neck scarves.

'*Très chic!*' encouraged Freda, as I fastened a floral-print silk kerchief around my neck. It does look fabulous, I thought, checking myself out in the mirror. But where would I wear it? Everyone else at work wore cheap suits or copies of designer fashions from Target or Kmart. But I just felt so special wearing it. Too bad, I thought, defiantly.

'I'll take it', I said to the cashier. 'Don't bother wrapping it. I'll wear it now.'

When I got back to the office, I showed Edith the kerchief. She thought it was beautiful and told me so. The next day, Freda went back to Myer and purchased a similar kerchief, which she wore around the office proudly.

'I hate it when she does this', Edith said to me privately.

'What, wears a scarf?' I asked.

'It's not just a scarf, it's an attitude', explained Edith. 'She does this all the time. She puts on a scarf and walks around the office like she is so much better than the rest of us. It's very sad. Who does she think she is, someone from *Lifestyles of the Rich and Famous*? Well she's not. She's just a lonely girl who never got married and doesn't know what to do with her money.'

I gulped, knowing full well that Edith was sending a not-so-subtle message to me.

Although Freda and I wore our scarves, despite the sniggers, Freda took hers off long before me. She started phasing it out in the lead-up to our trip to France and when we returned she never wore it again. Her scarf was stored in her cupboard along with all the clothes she bought in Europe—always in the background, but not a part of her day-to-day life.

★★★★

While I was nervous about continuing French lessons without the security of a friend, mostly I was disappointed and a little bit lonely. For a while I had thought that Freda shared the same dream and vision as me, but as I took myself off to the Alliance the first night of Beginners 2, I felt very much as though I was on my own.

Chapter 3
Learning verbs is one thing, speaking is another

The apostrophe

Je + voyelle = j'	*J'ai une voiture*
Je + he, hi, ho, hu, ha = j'	*J'habite en Australie*
Le, la + voyelle = l'	*l'avocat demande les questions*
Le, la + ha, he, hi, ho, hu = l'	*l'hésitation*

By Beginners 2 we were beginning to have committed to memory the present conjugations of the essential verbs: *être* (to be), *avoir* (to have), *faire* (to do) and *pouvoir* (to be able). In the present tense there are six different conjugations for every verb, so learning twenty-four different conjugations should have felt like an achievement. But it didn't, because although we could read them and write them, we couldn't say them or comprehend them.

We'd leave out the liaison when we spoke and when Sophie said anything that involved the use of the liaison she'd be met with a whole room of blank faces. One of the reasons that knowing French and actually understanding what the French are saying are two completely different things is because of the liaison. The liaison is employed whenever there is a word that begins with a vowel, and what it basically means is that the word will run directly on from the previous word, as though it was the one word.

The word *vous* (you), for example, is pronounced 'voo'. The word *avez* (have) is pronounced 'avay'. So, one would think that put them together to say 'you have' and they would sound something like 'voo-pause-avay'. Not so. Because *avez* starts with a vowel it runs on from the previous word. Oh, and there's a 'zzz' sound thrown in for good measure. So it actually sounds like 'voozavay'.

All of us had just assumed that if you knew the words and understood their meanings, you'd know French. We never realised that listening was going to be so tricky. It was frustrating. During class, one of the students muttered a comment about the 'damn French and their liaisons'.

Sophie smiled and switched to English. 'It is the fault of the French?' she asked. 'The other day my 'usband told me he was going to the shop to buy some bread. The words that are necessary to say this are: I, am, going, to, go, down, to, the, shops. Nine words. But what did he say? "I'm garn the shops." To me that sounds like four words.' She had a point.

Sophie's tales of learning English provided the class with light relief and some reassurance that others had been through what we were now struggling with. It also put pay to any complaints about the French language, because although it is a very difficult language to learn, English is much tougher.

'In French we don't have *this* or *that*, we just have *ce*', she told us. '*Ce* is this and *ce* is that. One day I was on the Geelong road with my 'usband. My 'usband was driving and I 'ad the map. We had to make a turn and so I yelled, "Get in this lane! Get in this lane!" And my 'usband was yelling, "What are you talking about? I am in this lane!" '

Although these stories were aimed at reassuring us, occasionally there were times when Sophie had a wicked gleam of pleasure in her eyes. Especially when it came to irregular verbs.

In most cases, you can roughly calculate what the conjugation of a verb is going to be from its infinitive form. The infinitive, *parler* (to speak), for example, is conjugated as *je parle, tu parles, elle parle* et cetera. *Manger* (to eat) is conjugated as *je mange, tu manges, elle mange*. In the case of irregular verbs, it's impossible to predict how the verb will be conjugated because the conjugations are nothing like the infinitive. *Être* (to be) is *je suis, tu es, elle est*. *Aller* (to go) is *je vais, tu vas, elle va*.

Often we would fall into the trap of trying to conjugate an irregular verb using the regular verb formation. '*Je alle ...*' we would stumble before Sophie smiled and corrected it to '*Je vais*'. On some occasions Sophie would smile her wicked smile and say, 'I had to do it. Now it's your turn.'

If the liaison hindered our understanding of Sophie's spoken French, the very minimal vocabulary we had after only a couple of semesters made it almost impossible.

'*Je suis allée au cinéma*', I stumbled, slowly. '*J'ai vu* The Spy Who Shagged Me ...'

'Ah,' Sophie smiled. 'Blah, blah, blah, blah ...'

I didn't understand a word she said.

'*C'est un film drôle, non?*' Sophie smiled.

It was obviously a question and the whole class was looking at me for a response, but I couldn't answer. My throat became tight, my tongue was made of concrete and there were a million thoughts racing through my head, none of which helped me construct an answer in French.

I was back at school again. High school or primary school, it didn't matter, it was always the same. In my perfect world, school would have been something like this: the students would sit in the class while the teacher taught them stuff; they would take notes, which they would study at home; then they would take a test and be graded. In fact, I think the reason why I achieved consistent high marks at university was because the lecture structure of university was just that.

At my school they valued class participation. I rarely volunteered to answer questions in class, so invariably the teachers would call on me to answer particular questions. It wasn't that I was lazy—in fact, I was very studious. My silence was caused by a disabling fear that I would be humiliated in front of my classmates. And it was caused by my voice.

My mother believes that my soft voice is a result of suffering from extremely bad asthma as a child. 'You had such trouble breathing', she explained. 'It was impossible for you to put any strength behind the words you were saying.' This may be true, but I think my little voice had more to do with confidence. I knew that if I weren't so scared of how people would react to what I said, then I would be able to boom my sentences out with great force.

I met a speech therapist at a party once and he pretty much confirmed my theory. 'When your throat muscles are constricted', he explained, 'the level of sound becomes weakened and the pitch becomes higher.

You need to learn how to relax your throat and speak from the depths of your lungs'. He gave me his card and offered to help me, but later on that night he hit on me. I refused, he called me Mickey Mouse and that was the end of that.

'Drôle', Sophie repeated more slowly. 'C'est un film drôle?'

I understood the words 'It's a film', but I had never heard this word *drôle* before.

'Drôle?' I responded, hoping that my puzzled, yet deeply thoughtful expression would tell Sophie that I didn't understand the word.

'Drôle', she responded forcefully. 'Drôle!'

I could feel my face become hot and flushed. Why couldn't French teachers understand that if you don't know the meaning of a word, it doesn't matter how many times they yell it at you? I won't understand the translation unless they tell me, I thought to myself angrily.

'Drôle?' I asked again, feebly.

At that moment another woman asked, 'Qu'est-ce que c'est drôle?'

'Funny', answered Sophie.

Great, I thought, now I can answer the damn question. Unfortunately, by this stage I was so rattled that I could barely utter the very basic 'Oui, c'est un film très drôle' without stuttering.

I did learn a valuable lesson though. *Qu'est-ce que c'est* … When you don't know what a word is, just ask. Sure, it sounds pretty obvious, but when you learn another language, you are not actually expected to comprehend every word. You start off recognising maybe one or two words of a question and as your comprehension improves you find that you can understand more and more of what is being said. My problem was that I was waiting for that improvement to kick in. I always thought that asking for a blow-by-blow translation was a bad thing—it meant you were avoiding training your ear. I had to learn that asking for a translation when I didn't know what a word might mean and couldn't understand an entire sentence, was not a cheats way out.

During that lesson I recognised I was at my usual drop-out point. I felt humiliated and the work was no longer easy. From here I would be required to work hard and put my dignity on the line every week.

When I got home I checked my emails. I had been subscribing to job-seeking websites for several months and it had quickly become clear from the lack of emails I was receiving that there were very few jobs for journalists advertised. There were considerably more advertised jobs for writers in the corporate world, but I didn't want to trade in my job at Moonlite for more of the same. I still believed there was a job out there that was interesting and exciting and would allow me to express my creativity.

That night, to my surprise, there was an email from SEEK, advertising a position as a journalist with a new online women's magazine called gURLpool.com.au. I sent off my CV and my standard covering letter.

★★★★

At the end of the semester break my spirits lifted. gURLpool.com.au called me in for an interview and suddenly the French lessons became easier, thanks to our new teacher, Patrice-Bertrand.

Patrice-Bertrand, or *Plastique*, as he came to be known, was typical of what Freda and I called a 'dopey-sack Frenchman'. He was tall, skinny and dressed like an uncool uni student. I don't think he ever reconciled with himself that he was actually a teacher, and whenever he explained something to the class he would giggle like a girl. You could imagine him loving French pop music.

Plastique had a very relaxed attitude towards learning French, which was quite a departure from Sophie and Xamuel. While they would correct every verb conjugation and have students repeating words until they pronounced them correctly, *Plastique* was happy if you had a go and blissful if you happened to get it correct.

Unit 5 was called *Ma Ville* (my town) and basically it consisted of learning how to give directions. What was such a relief about this class was that there were absolutely no verbs to learn, just straight vocabulary. A few key phrases were all we needed to learn: *vous tournez à droite* (you turn right), *vous tournez à gauche* (you turn left), *vous continuez jusqu' à la fin* (you continue to the end) and *vous traversez* (you cross).

The only time it became a little bit tricky was when we had to describe where something was situated, and again that was just a case of learning the vocab: *dans* (in), *à côté de* (next to) and *entre A et B* (between A and B).

Betrand's classes were not just easier, they were fun. In every class, Patrice-Bertrand handed out a photocopy of a map and we would go around the class, Patrice-Bertrand saying, 'I am at the town hall, tell me how to get to the library', or something similar. Other times he would pass out a shopping list and we would have to describe how we go from one shop to another to buy all the items.

Patrice-Bertrand's girlie laugh served to enhance his goofiness. When we returned to classes the following semester, we learnt that during the break Patrice-Bertrand was at a party when he fell from the balcony, breaking both his legs. His partner was none too pleased with this act of goofiness. She was nine months pregnant and Patrice-Bertrand was of no use to her with casts on both legs.

★★★★

At the beginning of every term there would be a whole new batch of students. They would all start off full of enthusiasm, trepidation and also optimism that they were on their way to being bilingual. Then, after a couple of lessons, one or two would drop out. By the end of the semester there would be, at the most, four people left in the class. At the beginning of the following semester, none would return, and there would be a whole new batch.

Chapter 4
Margie leaves for gURLpool

My country

Venir de (to come from)	*Je viens d'Australie*
Aller à (to go to)	*Je vais à Paris*
Être à (to be in)	*Je suis à Melbourne*

My interview with gURLpool was scheduled for 9am Wednesday. Before I left home I rang and left a message on Edith's voicemail saying that my partner of six years, Lincoln, was sick and I was taking him to the doctor and would be in late. I knew already that there would be dramas. At Moonlite, any time off at all was considered necessary only in the case of emergency, and should the emergency not be considered dire enough, staff members—even those not in your department— would be bitching about favouritism and slackness for weeks.

When I first saw Sarah, the editor of gURLpool, I thought she was possibly *the* most glamorous woman I had ever met. Tall, with long, blonde hair and big brown eyes, she was unquestionably beautiful. But it was the way in which she carried herself that stunned me. She was wrapped in a pink pashmina and gestured elegantly with long, manicured hands. She told me that she had worked for an entertainment magazine in the United Kingdom and currently wrote a column for a British women's magazine, essentially about life as a single woman. As she talked about what kind of articles I would be expected to write for gURLpool—fashion, food, entertainment, career, pregnancy and baby—I knew this was the job for me.

As expected, I received an icy welcome when I got back to Moonlite. 'Nice of you to join us', said Edith, a serious look on her face.

'Is everything okay?' I asked, putting my bag down at my desk.

'I don't know', Edith replied. 'David is in and I think he might have needed to see you about something, but then he wouldn't have been able to, would he? Seeing as you weren't here.'

I thought back to Sarah, her glamour, her enthusiasm for her craft and the job she had described that would see me out of the office for hours every day, interviewing exciting people and attending interesting events, and I began to get cross.

'By the way,' said Edith, turning away, 'your pay is being docked two hours'.

'What?' I cried. 'Lincoln was sick! You are allowed to take time off when a relative is sick. It's the law!'

'Family members', Edith replied smugly. 'You're allowed time off for family members. You and Lincoln are not married, and he is therefore not a family member.' Edith had always had a problem with the fact that Lincoln and I were not married. Not that she had a moral stance. It was more that she viewed my rejection of marriage as an insult to her choice of marrying. She turned her back on me and began typing on her computer.

Although I was shaking with rage, I said nothing. Stay calm, I thought, let's deal with this rationally. After a few minutes, I typed out an email to the payroll officer alerting her without emotion to the fact that my supervisor was threatening to dock my pay. Wasn't that, I asked, discrimination on the basis of marital status?

Yes, the payroll officer responded, and my pay could not be docked. She would handle it if the issue were put to her, which it hadn't been. Although I was relieved, I was still pissed off. That afternoon, Sarah sent me an email offering me the job and telling me that she would send through the contract in the next couple of days. As I was to be the first journalist employed, they hadn't yet drafted a contract.

I was excited and thrilled but, unexpectedly, terrified. While I was becoming increasingly frustrated with Moonlite, there was a certain amount of security attached to working there. I had produced the bi-monthly magazine and monthly newsletter enough times to know exactly what was involved, how much time I needed to do it and who provided me with what. And I was personally interested in health and fitness so writing the articles was, at times, stimulating.

Yet it was never exciting. I never spoke to anyone interesting and never left the office. Moonlite had taught me a lot about the process of publishing, but first and foremost I thought of myself as a writer and journalist.

What was unnerving was the unknown. Until now, all the magazine work I had done had been freelance. I had no idea how a magazine operated. How would I think up story ideas? How would I get interviews? When I turned up in the morning, what would I do?

I had heard people who worked at Moonlite praise the organisation by using phrases like 'a job for life'. At the time I remembered thinking, being in the same job all your life, schlepping out here every day, you reckon that's a good thing? But I was beginning to understand what they meant. If I wanted to, I could stay at Moonlite forever. It wasn't hard work. People liked me and the company was financially secure. There was the occasional upset, but overall, it was a non-stressful existence.

gURLpool, on the other hand, was a start-up. Okay, it had investors, but what if it didn't take off? What if there was no advertising and I was out on the street in a couple of weeks?

I emailed Sarah back and thanked her for the offer, telling her that I was thrilled to accept, but I was concerned about the financial security of the job, especially as I was leaving a job to come to gURLpool. No problem, she responded, she would get the CEO, Amy, to call me and explain the situation.

I went downstairs to get a coffee and Margie, the customer service manager, was sitting by herself in the tearoom reading a magazine. Margie was considered the mother hen of Moonlite. People from all over the organisation came to her with their problems, knowing she would listen sympathetically, offer good, solid advice, highlight all the attributes that made them a wonderful human being and leave them feeling good about themselves once more.

'Hi Mags,' I said, rinsing my cup.

'Hi Mags', Margie responded, flipping a page.

'Can I tell you something highly confidential?' I asked, sitting down opposite her. That got her attention, because there were very few things Margie liked more than a good gossip.

'I've been offered a job!' I said.

'Wow, that's great!' Margie smiled. 'Is it a job that you want? Is it doing the sort of thing you are doing now?'

'Sort of', I said. 'It's working as a journalist with a women's magazine.'

Margie looked as though she was about to cry with joy. 'Oh Mags, that's wonderful. I am so happy for you. You'll be so happy. What did Edith say when you told her? When do you start?'

'Well, I haven't told Edith yet because I haven't officially accepted the job. You know, it's a start-up company, I don't know how long it will be in business for …'

The smile fell from Margie's face and for the first time in two years I saw an angry Margie. 'Mags,' she said seriously, 'I'm only going to say this once: stop being a fucking idiot and go and resign'. I was shocked. Margie had never spoken to me in any way other than sweet and encouragingly.

'But …'

'Mags. I have listened to you talk about leaving for the past two years. You talk about your job like it's a stepping stone in your career, not just something that pays the bills. What, has something changed? Or was that just talk? If you don't accept this job, I'll, I'll, I'll … Well, I won't want to know you.' She picked up her magazine and continued reading.

I picked up my coffee and went back upstairs to Freda's office. 'Freddy, I need your help.' I took a deep breath. 'I have never done this before, so could you please help me write my letter of resignation?'

Chapter 5
Women who want to be French but miss the mark

My travels

prendre l'autobus	to take the bus
aller-retour	round trip
un siège côté couloir	aisle seat
un siège côté fenêtre	window seat
valise	suitcase

The train ride from Charles de Gaulle airport to Paris is pretty grim; endless suburbs of run-down houses and commission flats, which looked grey and dull in the early morning. We were excited about being in Paris—just to get off the damn plane was a relief—but it was a low-key start.

Despite the train ride, I was thrilled the moment we stepped off the plane. The smell of smoke and indoor heating, the French voices and advertising posters with half-naked women, the smell, the look—Paris was everything I remembered.

Freda hijacked the map and after a couple of minutes knew where we were going. Once we got off the Metro and the girls saw all the old buildings with the iron lacework, the cafes and the unfamiliar street signs, they perked up. But what really affected my friend Ky was when we turned the corner and found ourselves looking straight down the park to the Eiffel Tower.

Ky and I had been friends since we met at uni, but in the two years since our graduation our friendship had begun to peter out. We met for dinner a couple of times a year and then didn't communicate for months. It was during one of these dinners that I mentioned that Freda and I were going to Paris for the Millennium. Ky, who was bored with her job as an office assistant and irritated by living at home, told me immediately that she wanted to come with us.

I was a little surprised—I really didn't know her very intimately and she didn't know Freda at all. Plus, Ky had always struck me as a little bit shy and had been insecure about leaving uni for the real world. I thought she would have been terrified at the prospect of travelling to Europe with two people who were almost strangers. But there was just something about Paris—I knew it when she saw the Eiffel Tower for the first time.

Ky was speechless. It finally hit her that she was in the French capital. She could not stop smiling. Even Freda, whose enthusiasm was marred by a strong desire to put down her enormous suitcase and get a coffee, was driven to hug the two of us.

We only had a couple of hours until we were supposed to meet Aussie Bogan at Gare du Nord. We just had enough time to find the hotel, check in and sigh blissfully at our very Parisian rooms, with their tiny iron balconies, thick velvet curtains and gold embossed wallpaper. The hotel was by no means five star, but it was certainly quaint and, more importantly, just what we expected rooms in Paris to look like. The three of us giggled like schoolgirls who suddenly found themselves immersed in the most romantic city in the world.

'Check out the attitude', Freda muttered to me when we saw Aussie Bogan step off the Eurostar. You couldn't *miss* the attitude. Aussie Bogan stepped off the train with her chest puffed out and her head turning briskly from side to side as if to say, 'Well, I'm here, where are you?'

From the minute she met us, Aussie Bogan set about establishing the idea that Paris was her city and we were just unsophisticated tourists from Australia. True, Aussie Bogan had lived in Europe for a year, first of all in Dublin and then in London. But she had only stayed in Paris before and never lived there. In fact I had been to Paris many more times than her but it didn't matter. Aussie Bogan was the cosmopolitan one and we didn't have a clue, at least according to her.

She didn't need to consult a map, she knew what to order from a restaurant and how to do it and she knew the best places to go and spoke of the French with the fondness of an old friend. And she marched through the crowds in the Metro like it didn't faze her at all.

This wasn't the Aussie Bogan that Freda and I had befriended when we all attended the same yoga class in a Melbourne gym. That Aussie Bogan was sweet and funny. That Aussie Bogan always treated other people with kindness and respect. This Aussie Bogan was almost unrecognisable.

The four of us were already thinking about our post-New Year's Eve trip to Barcelona and Freda, Ky and I had started collecting information about getting there. By the time we met up with Aussie Bogan, we had settled on catching a *couchette* to Barcelona—it was cheaper than flying, plus we would save a night's accommodation. Tickets had to be booked at Gare du Nord and, as we were already going there to meet Aussie Bogan, we figured we'd book when we met her.

'What?' Aussie Bogan said looking at us as though we were peasants. 'You don't do that!'

Freda explained to her that a *couchette* was the cheapest option and Aussie Bogan shook her head in disbelief—and then took over. Couchettes are for tourists, Aussie Bogan explained. Real Europeans go directly to the airline and book the cheapest flights on offer. Although we weren't convinced that this was true, we followed Aussie Bogan to the Air France office at *l'Opéra*. Maybe she was right, but regardless, we didn't want to be treated like idiots.

After finding the office and then waiting in line for almost an hour, we discovered that it was, in fact, more than twice the price of a *couchette* to fly, so we trekked back to Gare du Nord to book a *couchette*. Unfortunately, that didn't diminish Aussie Bogan's superior attitude.

The irony of it, of course, was that Aussie Bogan was more of an Australian and more of a tourist than the rest of us. Even if it comes across as unfriendly, you admire the French women for their confidence and assertiveness. There was nothing to admire about Aussie Bogan. Her bad attitude didn't stem from pride and assertiveness like the Parisians', it was just schoolyard bully tactics. She was the stereotypical Aussie abroad. She wasn't interested in immersing herself in French culture, she just wanted to go to a pub where she could be with other English-speaking patrons and get pissed.

And, of course, she lacked the one vital ingredient required to pass as a native. Aussie Bogan had no sense of style. From her off-the-rack clothes to her plastic handbags, Aussie Bogan was never at risk of being mistaken for a Parisian. And her friend, British Bogan, was even worse.

British Bogan came over to Paris with Aussie Bogan, just for the one night, Millennium Eve. Aussie Bogan, Freda and I had met British Bogan during a yoga class while she was in Australia on holiday. Aussie Bogan kept in touch with British Bogan and the two became close friends when Aussie Bogan moved to the UK. British Bogan's gelled-back hair, orange make-up and skin-tight jeans said it all.

British Bogan was excited to show us a dress that she had purchased at some ridiculous price especially for New Year's Eve. We were excited about seeing it, too; it sounded magnificent. The dress was high necked and fell just below the knee. It was horrible. It was covered in hideous chunky bits of plastic that were supposed to look like jewels but instead looked like junk. British Bogan told us it was made from the finest raw silk, but it was covered in a sheen that made it look like it had already had a lifetime's wear. Plus, it was short-sleeved; not exactly appropriate for standing next to the Eiffel Tower in the middle of the night in the dead of winter.

The difference between Aussie Bogan and British Bogan was that there was nothing nasty about British Bogan. British Bogan tried to make friends with the rest of the group by having conversations with us and she never tried to dominate. However, it didn't stop Aussie Bogan from treating British Bogan badly.

Whenever Aussie Bogan fired a demeaning remark at Freda, Ky or myself and it failed, she would turn her venom on British Bogan. She'd scoff at anything British Bogan said or roll her eyes. British Bogan had come to spend New Year's Eve with people she didn't know, and we tried to include her. We kept our opinions about her fashion sense to ourselves, unlike Aussie Bogan, who on discovering our thoughts on her sense of style, decided to distance herself from her friend.

Aussie Bogan had a problem with the fact that Freda and I had taken French classes. It was the greatest threat to her 'I'm more French than you' plan, because Aussie Bogan didn't have a word of French. So she adopted the tactic favoured by those who consider their self-image to be threatened—mockery.

'Go on Margie, ask her if she has this skirt in an Australian size 16 but with a shorter hem and with a different pattern', she urged me when we visited the shopping centre Galleries Lafayette. I didn't know where to begin. If the sales assistant wanted to have a conversation about what we each did for a living and where we lived, I'd be fine. If she wanted directions to the other side of town, I'd have no problem at all helping her.

Je voudrais une jupe', I said slowly to the sales assistant, who nodded encouragingly. '*Mais, avec une ... um ... hem ... um, shorter ...*' The smile began to drop from the girl's face and she stopped nodding.

'Forget it', Aussie Bogan scoffed and returned the skirt to the rack. 'And I don't know if you should spend any more money on those French lessons!'

Aussie Bogan aimed to wound, and she did. She realised that my reluctance to speak had to do with a lack of confidence and she rode it for all it was worth. But it highlighted to me the misunderstanding that exists between those who are learning another language and those who aren't.

There is an assumption that when learning a language, you start at the general and then work your way up to the more specific. People think that if you are learning at the beginner's level you have a basic understanding of every aspect of the language; you just have to listen harder and it might take you longer to put together a response than it would for someone who was more advanced. The reality, though, is quite different.

The first year or so of learning another language involves developing an understanding of the tenses. From there, you add vocab, idioms, et cetera. You start by learning very specific details, and then move to the broader concepts of making yourself understood.

From Beginners 1 to Beginners 2, we had learnt all there is to know about the present tense and verb conjugation—none of which is particularly useful in situations other than introductions or descriptions. And at that stage your vocab is extremely limited. You might know the six different conjugations of the verb 'to have' but have no clue as to what a hem or a pattern is.

Aussie Bogan wasn't the only person who wore Paris as a badge of honour. Such is the mystique and mythology of the city that some women think that by claiming it as their own, somehow the glamour and beauty will become part of their own personality. This manifests itself in a couple of ways. In the case of Aussie Bogan, she adopted the know-it-all approach. She knew where to shop, how to order from the menu and how to navigate the Metro. Of course, we did too, only we never got the opportunity to show it. Whenever plans were to be made Aussie Bogan jumped in and took over, thereby establishing herself as the Paris Woman.

Another, less subtle way of aligning oneself with Paris is to not only announce yourself as Paris Woman, but to tell everyone else they are not. That was the tactic employed by Butterfly Butcher (nicknamed because she collected exotic, dead butterflies). Butterfly Butcher lived in New York and came over to spend New Year's Eve with us in Paris. While we were there, she wasn't as forceful—even she could not compete with Aussie Bogan's mission—but she demonstrated her very own mission in a letter I received not long after I returned home.

She started off by explaining that she was writing me a letter because she had some news to break to me. I thought, my God what could have happened? 'I've got a transfer and I'm going to be living in Paris', she wrote. 'I know you love Paris and you're probably a bit jealous that it is me who is going to be living there and not you, but I just want you to know that I wish you were here too and I hope you don't hate me.'

My reaction was a cross between anger and bewilderment. The letter was a thinly disguised gloat and you didn't need half a brain to read between the lines: you poor pathetic thing, I am the star living your dream. It was a lot less than what I expected from a friend. Imagine if

I really did feel that way about Paris? I would have been shattered by that letter.

And that was the point. I did love Paris, but I never said I wanted to live there, because I didn't. She had either assumed that everyone felt the same need to claim ownership of Paris or she was just looking for a cheap shot. I loved Paris and adored being there, but I wasn't deluded enough to think that everyday life in Paris was a bed of roses. I knew if I actually had to work and support myself in Paris, I wouldn't last.

And neither could Butterfly Butcher apparently, because after a few months of being pushed around on the Metro, making no friends and spending her entire wage on rent, Butterfly Butcher decided to move back to New York.

Chapter 6
The girls celebrate Millennium Eve in Paris

Indications of time

Le passé:	*avant*	before
	hier	yesterday
	la semaine passée	last week
Le présent:	*maintenant*	now
	en ce moment	at the moment
	aujourd'hui	today
Le futur:	*après*	after
	demain	tomorrow
	la semaine prochaine	next week

Underneath Paris there is an extensive network of tunnels, dug deep into the ground. The Paris catacombs were originally constructed as a place to throw dead bodies once the graveyards were full and were extended and used during the Second World War as hiding places for Resistance fighters. These days the catacombs are a major tourist attraction.

Tourists come to the catacombs because of their gruesome history; to experience what it must have been like for the tunnel dwellers. In a way that can only be described as very French, the authorities have taken a creative approach to combining horror with the aesthetically pleasing. Skulls placed on top of each other line the walls from floor to ceiling, kilometre after kilometre. Grey to almost white empty eye sockets stare out at the tourists as they walk past. Darker coloured skulls have been strategically placed to form decorative patterns, or act as feature items, shaped as crosses or skirting boards.

'Death as decoration.' Butterfly Butcher shuddered. 'How awful!' Ky thought this was a particularly amusing comment coming from a woman who has dead butterflies pinned behind glass on the walls of her apartment.

We waited in line for an hour before we were able to enter the catacombs, so we could only imagine what the line is like during the peak summer holiday period. As we went down the stairs it became colder, darker and more damp. Down and down we went before we entered the tunnels.

There's not a lot to do in the catacombs except express your horror at all the skulls. After that it's just a case of walking—a macabre kind of promenade. Being so deep underground, the floors were wet and the dust from the deteriorating skulls formed a grey-coloured mud that covered our shoes. We called it Dead People Mud.

The first thing we did when we got back to the hotel was scrub the Dead People Mud off our shoes, it was revolting. The scary thing was that the next morning, the day of Millennium Eve, our shoes were still covered in it. Apparently Dead People Mud is almost impossible to remove.

Freda and Aussie Bogan joked that the catacombs were full of Madame's friends, she was that old. Madame would often appear at breakfast with her wig on crookedly, scuttling around serving huge bowls of coffee and chocolate and carrying trays of crusty baguettes and pots of jam from the kitchen. My brother Geoff and his wife Lisa, who had recently stayed at the same hotel, called her The Duck because when she spoke she sounded like she was quacking. And she spoke a lot, not seeming to care or understand that none of us spoke French.

Madame slept in the front bedroom of the hotel and had probably done so for fifty years. Every morning she was the first to rise to take delivery of the bread, and breakfast was ready and waiting for us no matter what time we got up. Madame would always be there, smiling and chuckling to herself.

Madame's breakfasts were legendary. Everyone who experienced them felt the same way. It wasn't like eating at a hotel, guests felt as though they were at Madame's home instead, being lavished with bread and fresh jam, chocolate and coffee by their own Grandma.

★★★★

The excitement and anticipation of the dawning of a new millennium was fanned by a fear that was gripping the entire world: the Y2K bug. According to conspiracy theorists, leading bankers and computer gurus, at exactly twelve midnight civilisation as we knew it was going to end.

Y2K panic was caused when the people who invented and developed computers didn't anticipate the year 2000. Programs that controlled world finance, internal infrastructure like electricity and water, and air traffic and weapons of mass destruction, only had two digits to signify the year. The theory was that when it ticked over to 00, these computers would 'think' it was the beginning of time and cease to operate. The fact that computer systems were built on top of other systems meant the problem was not easily rectified. To change the date on every program would involve literally rewriting all the code ever cut.

At best, we were told, it would mean no essential services like water and electricity, no food being delivered and no way to get money out of the bank. People were stocking up on bottled water and canned food and some, fearing anarchy, moved their families out into the bush. At worst, they said, it would be the end of the world.

The scary thing was, it wasn't just the doomsday prophets who were preaching that the end was nigh. Airlines refused to have planes in the air at midnight. The annual leave of all serving police officers in countries like Australia, England and France was cancelled. Even the Australian government was officially in session all night, so no parliamentarians were allowed to drink a drop of alcohol. The world was on high alert. And we were about as far away from home as it is possible to be.

At four o'clock in the afternoon we joined the Parisians as they switched on their televisions and radios to see if Australia and New Zealand still existed. Australia and New Zealand were the first countries to move into the new millennium, Europe followed eight hours later.

Freda, Ky and I spent the late afternoon getting ready and watching the coverage of the New Year celebrations back home. The country hadn't fallen into disarray and Australians were enjoying the fireworks over the Harbour Bridge in Sydney and the river parade in Melbourne.

Ky was sitting on my bed watching TV when she suddenly got up and said, 'I've got a surprise for you'. She disappeared into her room and came out holding three champagne glasses—one for each of us. The stems of the glasses were clear and contained the number 2000 in gold, surrounded by gold glitter. She had brought them all the way from Australia. Freda popped the champagne and we had our own pre-New Year's Eve celebration. We were in Paris at a very momentous time in history. It was emotional for all three of us.

The beauty of the moment was shattered by a phone call from Aussie Bogan, who was in a room down the hall. 'Hey!' she said. 'British Bogan's just discovered an Aussie Bar nearby and we reckon we should go there tonight?'

Getting pissed in a bogan Australian theme bar was not how we had planned to spend Millennium Eve in Paris. We didn't go to bogan pubs in Australia and we certainly hadn't travelled to the other side of the world to start. 'Ah, I'll talk to the girls about it', I said and hung up.

Ky and Freda would have laughed if they hadn't been so horrified. 'What are we going to do?' wailed Ky.

With Freda on board, we needn't have worried. 'Look,' she said assertively, 'we tell them what we are doing and if they don't want to join us, if they want to go off and do something else, let them. If they want to stay with us, that's fine too. We're not going to be told what to do tonight'.

Just at that moment, my Aunty Jan called as she had said she would. Jan, her daughter Lisa and Lisa's daughter Rachael make up the stylish side of the family. All three women are intelligent, sophisticated and very cosmopolitan. It surprised no-one in my family when Jan announced she was taking Rachael to Paris for Millennium Eve. Jan looked as though she could have been Rachael's mother; they both had children when they were very young.

Part One: Beginners

47

Jan was staying at a friend's apartment in Paris and wanted us to come over for some champagne and food. The girls had been to the market that day and were creating a seafood buffet that they were going to enjoy on the roof, which had breathtaking views of the city.

Freda picked up the phone and dialled Aussie Bogan's room. 'Hi, it's Freda', she said with her no-nonsense voice. 'Margie tells me you're thinking of going to an Aussie theme bar ...' That was followed by a giant pause only interrupted with Freda's 'mmm', as Aussie Bogan explained the knee-slapping, rip-roaring time they foresaw at the pub.

'Right', said Freda eventually. 'That sounds good. Here's what Margie, Ky and I are going to do: we're going to have champagne and food near the Louvre and then we are going to walk along the Seine to the Eiffel Tower and watch the fireworks. You guys are welcome to join us if you like.'

After a quick consultation with British Bogan, they decided they'd come with us. As we walked to the first *arrondissement* we saw people out on the street, but while the atmosphere was electric, there was none of the aggression and violence that seems to accompany similar large public events in Australia. When we got to the Louvre, we called Jan and she came and got us. Her friend Denis's apartment was small but it opened onto a huge balcony, which was actually a rooftop, and the views were incredible. The Eiffel Tower was lit up and a searchlight at the top of it roamed the city.

Rachael and Jan had prepared some gorgeous seafood, which we ate with our champagne. Rachael was enjoying playing the hostess and flitted from guest to guest. She loved the whole Paris experience. She was dressed in a white cardigan with white fur cuffs and whenever someone commented on how lovely she looked in it, she would flick her hair and say, 'I got it in Paris'.

It was great to see British Bogan enjoying herself and she loved Jan and Rachael. Even Aussie Bogan was pleasantly surprised at how much fun classy could be.

Just after eleven we left Jan's and walked back along the Seine to the Eiffel Tower. The streets were packed but the mood remained more festive than threatening. There were a couple of frightening elements though.

'Guys,' said Ky seriously, 'we've got some trouble back here'.

Paris is notorious for its street crime and everything pointed to New Year's Eve as being a bad, bad night. Tourists were pouring into the capital and so were the bogans from the suburbs, ready to cause trouble. The situation was made all the more dangerous by the fact that the Metro was closing not long after midnight—leaving a lot of drunk, tired people with nowhere to go.

We'd all made a pact that should one of us get into any sort of trouble, we'd all stick together and help. Now Ky was sounding the call. Evidently, she had felt someone tugging at the day pack she had on her back and she wanted to sort the problem out before there was one.

We turned around and saw that there was not one person pulling at her bag, there were about three of them. Which could have been very serious—except the kids couldn't have been older than about eight. And they didn't want to rob Ky; they wanted to play with her. Of course, Ky had done the right thing by alerting us to possible trouble, but that didn't stop us teasing her for the rest of the night. We even coined a phrase for Ky's affliction—infantaphobia—an irrational fear of children.

During our Millennium trip, we only experienced violence once, and it wasn't at the hands of drunken youths from the suburbs. Standing in the Metro on New Year's Day, a gentleman trying to get past me picked me up by the shoulders and threw me onto an empty magazine stall. When I picked myself up I turned to look at the culprit, expecting a youth or some person on the fringe of society who had no manners. What I saw was a very respectable-looking middle-aged man, dressed in a suit and carrying a briefcase.

What scared me the most on New Year's Eve were the fireworks that were being launched into the crowds. Being Australian, I had been brought up to fear fireworks. I had heard all my life that there was a damn good reason why they are illegal. Children get maimed and killed. Those things are as lethal as a loaded gun.

Now I was in a city packed with people who were armed with loaded guns and not afraid to use them. Every so often a patch of street would suddenly clear and we'd know that someone had released a Catherine wheel across the ground. Or we'd hear a whizzing noise and would duck, hoping that whatever it was wouldn't land anywhere near us.

The only person more scared of the amateur pyrotechnics than me was Aussie Bogan. We found a spot very close to the side of the Eiffel Tower, in-between a barrier and a house. From there we had a clear and close view of the tower and we were safe and removed from the swarm of people passing us. At one stage, a firework was released very close to us and in her panic Aussie Bogan crashed through the barrier into the crowds.

The Millennium Clock attached to the Eiffel Tower had been up for a year and counted down the days, hours and minutes to the new millennium. It broke three hours before midnight. But that was okay, the tower was glittering and looked beautiful. It was a clear balmy night and the fireworks were the most amazing I had seen in my life—the sky lit up like the daytime and sparks poured out of the tower. I am sure every person in Paris that night felt the same as me, but I was convinced—this was the dawning of a very special time.

Chapter 7
Aleksandra, the most glamorous of teachers

The past tense

Formulation of the past tense:

subject + present form of avoir/être + past participle of verb

For example:

Je suis allé	I went
Tu as travaillé	You worked
Vous avez lu le livre	You read the book

Our trip to France for Millennium Eve fell in the summer holidays in Australia, so I didn't miss any of my French classes. On the first day of the new semester, I was introduced to a new teacher, Aleksandra, and a class full of new students.

Aleksandra had to be the sexiest teacher at the Alliance. She presented herself well, all her clothes were fashionable and the ensembles put together perfectly, from the leopard print top to the exquisite ankle boots, and her hair and make-up were arranged to make her look the best she could without appearing to have tried. Aleksandra enjoyed a good flirt with the male teachers and students and split her sides at smutty jokes. She was probably in her early fifties and she oozed sex appeal.

Perhaps because she was the oldest teacher we had thus far, she also commanded a great deal of respect from the students. Aleksandra was a true French woman, glamorous and dignified, who scoffed at anything that wasn't cultural, fashionable or intelligent. She absolutely refused to speak in English and would continue to speak in French no matter how long it took for the class to understand a point.

Stormin', whose real name was Norman, one of the new students, was smitten. Beginners 4 was Stormin's first class at the Alliance and from the snippets of information he let drop from time to time, we found out that he was divorced, retired and lived above a pub in St Kilda. Apparently he had been to France, had a 'bloody good time' and decided he would spend his spare time learning French. When he turned up for class and saw Aleksandra he thought he had hit the jackpot.

Stormin' would have been in his fifties, and judging by his weathered appearance, they were a rough fifty. His grey, oily hair hung around his face, which was covered by a large pair of glasses. His face looked like a road map and his teeth were yellow.

At first I thought he was too advanced for our class; he could reel off sentences in a row with a perfect accent and at a rapid speed. Most of the time we couldn't understand a word of what he was talking about. We soon worked out, though, that his French was grammatically very poor. He just had the accents and gestures to pull it off, and the courage to keep talking away in spite of all his errors.

The reason he did this was undoubtedly because he wanted to impress Aleksandra. He would spend the class staring and smiling at her, laughing a little too hard at her jokes and vehemently agreeing with everything she said.

'Ah, the croissant!' he would croon. 'Nobody makes the croissant like the French. The aroma! The freshness!' It went on and on.

'There are no women in the world as beautiful as the French women! You, Madame, are a vision!' He always called her madam and, despite his sleaziness, was always totally respectful of her.

He knew we all thought he was a freak, but that was the way he liked it. Anything to make him stand out to Aleksandra was perfectly fine by him. He wanted to look like he embraced everything French in the hope, I am sure, that the very French Aleksandra would one day embrace him. He revelled in the persona of the eccentric Francophile with the matching accent; he loved playing the game. Until the game got too hard.

Passé composé. To anyone who has ever tried to learn French, these two words strike fear in the heart. Put simply, the *passé composé* is the past tense. Up until this point, everything that we said was in the present: *Je suis journaliste, j'aime la musique française* et cetera.

The horror of the *passé composé* is that two verbs—both conjugated—have to be used together. The first verb is either *avoir* or *être* in its present form and the second verb is the one you want to use but in its past participle. For example, 'I spoke to Julie' would become *J'ai parlé à Julie*. 'I did the shopping' would become, *J'ai fait le shopping*. For those of us who had barely committed to heart the present conjugations of *avoir* and *être*, having to use them all the time and with another verb, was almost unimaginable.

Learning the *passé composé* is only achieved by using it regularly. So Aleksandra would begin every lesson by asking us to share what we had done in the past week. We soon discovered that there are phrases you use regularly and say enough that you forget that you are conjugating two verbs. You're just repeating a phrase.

'Je suis allé…' was was used regularly, as was *'J'ai travaillé'*. By the end of Beginners 4 we were using the *passé composé* regularly and with some ease. But sentences that involved verbs we didn't use all the time still drained our brains. The *passé composé* presented even more of a problem for Stormin'. He was struggling just as much as the rest of us, plus he was living in fear of looking stupid in front of Aleksandra.

To learn the *passé composé*, Aleksandra would hand out copies of text written in the present. One by one we would have to read aloud an example, changing the verb that was used to the *passé composé*. Sometimes it took a while. Adding the form of *avoir* or *être* was no longer a problem, but who knows by heart the passé form of a verb like *épier* (to spy upon)?

Considering Stormin's infatuation with Aleksandra, I was surprised that he stopped coming to class after only half a semester. But the humiliation factor had increased twofold in line with the two verb usage of *passé composé*, and Stormin' had more on the line. While all the students disliked embarrassing themselves in front of a room full of strangers, for Stormin' it was a catastrophe, as he was also embarrassed in front of the woman he was so eager to impress.

For me, the embarrassment had become just an obstacle on the road to where I wanted to go. Millennium Eve had convinced me that the glamorous life was available to me, and gURLpool had shown me that it was within my reach.

gURLpool was in a large open plan office situated in a run-down building in North Melbourne. Although the paint was peeling on the outside and the foyer had worn lino on the floor, the inside of gURLpool office was very modern (thanks to all those venture capitalists who were throwing money into dotcoms at the time), and exactly how I imagined a women's magazine to look.

As soon as someone walked in they were confronted by the receptionist's desk, decorated with an ornate flower arrangement, behind which was a huge illuminated logo of the magazine. The walls were a dark pink and the furniture—all new—was lightly coloured pine.

My desk was situated between Liz, the marketing manager, and Sarah, the magazine's editor. Sitting beside Liz was fun because, behind her elegant facade, she was essentially a dag, and someone who had the ability to see the funny side of almost every situation.

Sitting beside Sarah was another matter. I was the first full-time journalist employed by gURLpool, so I was plonked pretty much wherever the desk happened to be. As other journalists joined the magazine, a little section was established in the middle of the room. Yet, I remained where I was.

Because I was so close to the editor, and because at that stage I was willing to help out in any way I could, I gradually took on the role of assistant editor, as well as journalist. If Sarah was swamped with work, she would pass some over to me, be it proofing, selecting images or answering emails. Often when there was conflict between Sarah and another journalist, I would act as an intermediary.

Years later, another journalist who worked at gURLpool told me, somewhat bitterly, that the only reason I was promoted to editor when Sarah left was because I worked in such close proximity to her—and because I put up with all her crap.

Although every woman who worked at gURLpool was glamorous, Sarah looked and acted the star. Draped in a pashmina and tottering around on stilettos, she would look for a way to name-drop in every conversation. 'You chose the Egyptian linen? Nicole [Kidman] told me once that she and Tom [Cruise] have Egyptian linen.' Sarah had spent several years in London, writing for an entertainment magazine, so the casual stories of star-studded encounters were frequent.

It didn't take long to realise that Sarah didn't want to just report on stars—she wanted to be the star. gURLpool, being one of the first high-quality online magazine of its kind, was receiving a lot of press. In any given week, Sarah would appear with Amy, the CEO, in a magazine or newspaper speaking about the magazine. But it was never enough to satisfy her. More than once I had to lower my head and pretend to be engrossed in work, as Sarah gave Liz a tongue-lashing over how many times her name was mentioned in a press release, whether or not it was mentioned first or whose photo accompanied an article.

Although I never said anything, I did think that a lot of the animosity directed at Sarah was born from jealousy. Every woman who worked at gURLpool was glamorous, but Sarah was fabulous. Sarah didn't need to spend hours putting together her outfit for the day, because all her clothes were gorgeous. She was well travelled and very successful in her career. For the other women in the office, gURLpool was a dream because for the first time in their working lives they could be girlie and frivolous and discuss at length issues like the latest mascara, or what a certain supermodel had worn to a premiere over the weekend. But for Sarah, the dream was her reality.

I genuinely liked Sarah. She was very kind to me and normally very supportive. If anyone needed time off work for any reason she would accommodate them, and show concern at any personal problems her staff may have been experiencing. She often brought in small gifts as a gesture of thanks and once, after a particularly gruelling week, Sarah treated me and the other journalist to an afternoon at a day spa.

Plus, I knew I could learn a lot from Sarah. She had spent some years overseas and had written for a number of high-profile magazines and without question she was a very talented writer. Sarah recognised that I was eager to learn from her experience and we worked very closely together on many articles.

Sarah was not the least bit ashamed of what she called self-promotion, and it was this that the other staff members found unpalatable. It was true that she didn't always know when self-promotion crossed the line and hurt others.

In order for Sarah to be the star around the office, it was necessary for her to distinguish herself from everyone else. For the journalists, and me in particular, being the closest thing to an editor in waiting, this quirk manifested itself in correcting our errors vocally and loudly.

'Margie, I just don't understand this', she said one day while reading one of the stories I had written. 'Are you trying to be funny or is this just written sloppily?'

'Did you read this before you sent it to me?' was another one of her favourites.

As the office was always so quiet it was impossible for anyone not to hear and while it seemed to cause anger in the other journalists, for me it was just plain humiliating. The worst thing was trying to conduct interviews under these circumstances. These were early days at gURLpool, before public relations companies began offering interviews and we often had to cold call. It was always painful to me to phone someone who wasn't expecting the call, probably wasn't interested in talking to me, and was always highly suspicious.

'Hi there. My name is Margaret Ambrose and I am a journalist with gURLpool.com.au … It's an online magazine … Well, if you want you can check it out on the web. I believe you have created some stunning gardens and I would like to interview you for a story about interesting ways to pave … Yes, just a couple of quotes will do … No, we generally don't allow subjects to read articles before they are published … Well if you visit the site you can see that we are a reputable magazine.'

While this conversation was taking place, everyone in the office was listening, including Sarah, who was forthcoming with advice.

'You know, Margie,' she said, 'you should have told them that we are the number one online magazine in Australia. Why didn't you tell them the number of hits we get? Why didn't you tell them to read the article about us in today's *Leader* newspaper?'

Of course, I needed to be reassured, not savaged, but I said nothing. I had seen what happened to other journalists who questioned Sarah's judgment in front of the whole office (lots of screaming that always ended in Sarah firing off emails to staff and management about the incompetence of the woman), so I merely thanked her for her advice and set about writing.

Aside from these moments of tension, working at gURLpool was everything I had hoped it would be. Every day was different and exciting—interviewing celebrities, writing about popular culture, choosing what make-up or fashion to profile. It was exhilarating to be involved in putting together such a sexy, sassy women's magazine and my writing was gradually becoming more creative and edgy. I was at last being allowed, and even encouraged, to develop my own style.

Chapter 8
Margie and Julie learn how to express a desire

The subjective
Verb tense that is used when expressing a wish, desire, opinion.

Aller (to go)	... *que j'aille* (... that I go)
Avoir (to have)	... *que j'aie* (... that I have)
Être (to be)	... *que je sois* (... that I be)
Faire (to do)	... *que je fasse* (... that I do)

Classes at the Alliance were two hours long and there was a ten-minute *petite pause* (little break) in the middle. After concentrating so hard for an hour, it was a welcome relief and the chance to smoke a much needed cigarette.

There were three smokers in the class: me and two other girls, named Julie and Rachel. Rachel was in her early twenties and Julie was a little older, but they were the only people I had encountered since studying French who were, well, kind of like me.

What brought us together was a love of French, smoking and our mutual contempt for Norman. Rachel was a little bit shy, but Julie and I hit it off straightaway. While she desperately wanted to be able to speak French, I noticed in class that she also had a sense of humour and was able to laugh at herself, and me, when necessary.

Julie loved everything French, including movies, music and books. She was very attractive and was obsessed with fashion, which meant she was rarely seen walking into class without a copy of French *Vogue* under her arm.

From what I could tell, Julie was studying French for exactly the same reasons as me. She worked during the day performing data entry for a bank, while at night she was studying journalism. Julie had dreams of becoming a fashion journalist. She was convinced that journalism was a more glamorous career choice and she believed in the glamour of France, and she wanted both to be her reality.

I recognised the similarities between Julie and me straightaway. She too was quiet and a little timid. Her determination in classes didn't translate into forcefulness. She sat quietly and waited to be asked a question then she would respond slowly with a well thought out answer. She was at about the same level that I was and there were times I could tell that, like me, she really struggled. Yet, week after week she turned up by herself, which made me wonder what was driving her.

Despite her struggles with the language, Julie had an enthusiasm for all things French that was contagious and being around her on Thursday evenings was the only time I could be an unashamed Francophile.

'I bought you this', she said one night after class, handing me a small package. It was a bar of soap, wrapped in delicate brown paper and tied together with a small purple ribbon, with delicately ornate French words penned on it.

'It's beautiful', I gasped.

'I know,' sighed Julie, 'I got one for me too, but I don't know if I will use it. I might just put it in my bathroom so I can look at it every day'.

Which was exactly what I was thinking. The only difference was, around anyone else, I would have been hesitant to voice it. None of my friends had any interest in anything French. Ky and Freda had lapped it up while we were in France—arriving home with suitcases full of French clothes and make-up, and a resolve to be more French— but it hadn't taken them long to slip back into their Australian ways.

I, on the other hand, had held onto the idea with a passion. I hunted down the newsagents that stocked French magazines, stores that sold French beauty products and even food importers who stocked produce from France. And I was aware that it was a little bit embarrassing. One night I had the girls around for dinner and when I got up to change the CD I asked if there were any requests.

'I don't care, as long as it is in English!' Ky said. The others laughed and so did I, although I was blushing.

Lincoln, the man who shared my life and my house, never said anything about the Francophile turn our lives were taking. Sometimes I wondered if he thought it was a phase I would just grow out of but the truth was, he just didn't care all that much. If he was eating French food, it was just as good to him as anything else I would cook. If I chose to read French magazines it mattered no more to him than if I read *Cosmo;* and he didn't care if the cushions on the sofa were imported from Paris, as long as they continued to prop him up while he watched Sunday afternoon footy.

Only occasionally would he express some irritation. 'Margie, come here!' he yelled from the bathroom one morning. 'You need to come and find the shampoo for me.'

'It's on the shelf,' I yelled back.

'But I don't know which bottle it is,' he responded. 'They're all in goddamn French!'

Lincoln was a little troubled that I went to France for four weeks to celebrate the New Millennium while he stayed at home and worked, but he did his best not to show it. We had decided very early on in our relationship that we wouldn't be one of those couples that gave up their own interests and did everything together. I put up with it when he spent every Saturday during summer playing cricket, which I had no interest in, and he put up with it when I went overseas.

A lot of our friends had trouble understanding the way we chose to conduct our relationship, but we considered it to be very mature, and, as the years passed and we were still together, very wise.

★★★★

'Margie, guess what?' Julie said excitedly one Thursday night as we lit our cigarettes. 'I'm moving to Elwood!' Julie knew that I lived in Elwood from some of our conversations in class. She told me that her father had purchased an apartment in Elwood and had agreed to let Julie live there for minimal rent. Julie's excitement at moving to Elwood made me begin to be excited about the area I had lived in for five years.

Considering that we would now be living just a couple of streets from each other, we agreed that homework would be a lot more fun if we did it together at the weekend. We decided we'd meet at The Lounge, a groovy bar in Ormond Road and have a drink and nibble on dips and bread while we helped each other with our work. It started a tradition that lasted all through our time at the Alliance.

Perhaps it was the alcohol, or because we were studying the most troublesome tense in the French language, but when Julie and I got together at The Lounge to study, our homework suddenly got a massive injection of humour.

If you want anything in French you need to know *l'impératif* and *le subjonctif*. *L'impératif* is used to express an immediate request. *'Passez-moi le journal!'* (pass me the newspaper!) or *'Donnez-moi un stylo!'* (give me a pen!) *L'impératif* is not hard to understand, because it is very similar to the present form of the verb.

Le subjonctif gives every French student grief. *Le subjonctif* is used to express a desire, wish or doubt, so it is commonly used. The problem is, the conjugations look nothing like any others. *Aller*, for example, becomes *'j'aille'*, *être* becomes *'je sois'* and *pouvoir* becomes *'je puisse'*.

Conjugating in *le subjonctif* is not something one can guess. It's also not a verb tense that is easy to know when to use because it's not always easy to tell if something you are saying is a subjective expression.

One afternoon, Julie and I were sitting back on the comfy old couch in The Lounge and going through all the exercises Aleksandra had given us for homework. A couple of vodkas and tonic later and we were becoming a little bored. The final exercise, though, required us to use a little more imagination.

In the book there were ten small cartoons, drawn it seemed, by the same cartoonist who does the drawing for all foreign language text-books. The instructions were that we had to write the caption for each one using either *le subjonctif* or *l'impératif*.

The first cartoon showed a little boy up a tree and a mother standing below with a stern expression on her face. 'Come down immediately?' I suggested.

Julie slumped back in her chair. 'Yes,' she said, then a sly smile appeared on her face. 'Or, I hope you fall and break your neck!' After we'd stopped laughing and wiped the tears from our eyes we realised that we could write that. It was expressing a desire so we would be using the *subjonctif*. That was it. We decided to write a funny caption for all of them.

The picture of a ski instructor talking to a group of students became, 'One, two, three … I hope we didn't start with four'. The picture of a man behind a desk talking to another man became, 'Tell me why it is you want a sex change operation', and the image of a small boy at a movie theatre box office became, 'Give me two tickets to *Baise-moi*'. *Baise-moi* was a French film that caused a sensation when it was banned in Australia after one night because of its explicit sex and violence.

The outrageous answers Julie and I came up with became legendary in class and whenever Aleksandra would call on us she would have a huge smile on her face, anticipating our response. The only trouble was, sometimes we would be laughing so much we couldn't actually deliver our answers. With tears streaming down our faces we would try to spit them out, while the rest of the class strained to comprehend what we were saying.

Aleksandra didn't mind, in fact she encouraged our creativity. We knew why. By this stage we had seen many students come and go who were discouraged by the hard work and the humiliation. The fact that we could laugh at things—especially at ourselves—meant that we continued. And Aleksandra made the classes as entertaining as possible.

'My husband was sleazy when we first met', Aleksandra explained to us one day with an innocence that suggested she didn't quite understand the subtleties of the word sleazy. That wasn't surprising since we had introduced her to the word only moments before.

As a comprehension exercise we watched a short scene from a movie and Aleksandra asked us to explain what had happened. What happened was a sleazy man in a buttoned-down shirt and a pink jumper around his neck had approached a skimpily clad girl at a seaside restaurant and asked her to go out on a date with him.

'*Il est … qu'est-ce que c'est* sleazy?' asked Julie.

Aleksandra had a blank look. 'I don't know what this word is, sleazy?'

We tried to explain sleazy to Aleksandra, throwing up words like fake, predatory, even Pepe Le Peu, but Aleksandra remained expressionless. 'We don't have a word for this in French', she concluded.

'Yes, they do,' Julie muttered under her breath. 'Normal.'

To our surprise, Aleksandra agreed. 'My husband was sleazy when we first met', she stated. 'Wasn't yours?'

'No!' I said.

'But the first time he spoke to you he was, no?'

'No', I insisted.

'Well, how did you ever start to talk to him?'

'I was in the same class as him at university', I said.

Aleksandra shook her head and muttered something I didn't understand but which seemed to me to say, 'How boring, you poor thing'.

In the car on the way home Julie and I had a laugh about the video, and agreed that watching a guy try to pick up a girl sounds a whole lot more sleazy when it's being done in French.

'How's the whole blow-waved hair and jumper-tied-around-the-neck look!' I grimaced.

'Oh, I don't mind that', replied Julie. 'It's very ooh-la-la French.'

'Are you serious?' I laughed. 'It's horrible! It's so 1980s *Miami Vice*.'

I looked at Julie, in her expensive funky clothes that I knew would have come from the latest, hottest designer, and marvelled at her sudden lack of taste.

Julie shrugged, in a very French way. 'That's France', she sighed.

'You,' I said with mock seriousness, 'are obsessed.' I shook my head solemnly. 'Your obsession with France has gone so far as to override your obsession with fashion. And I never thought I'd see the day.'

That night, it occurred to me that my blossoming friendship with Julie had altered my whole experience of learning French. In the very beginning I stuck with my classes because of a strong desire to be able to speak French. I took myself off to class every Thursday more nervous than excited, worried about appearing foolish or stupid. Now I laughed in class, and laughed on the way home, and I didn't even care if a teacher teased me in class. Now, I was going because I was having so much fun.

Part Two:
Intermediate

Chapter 9
Butchering the language

Expressing an opinion

Je trouve que …	I find that …
Selon moi …	According to me …
Je crois que …	I believe that …
Je pense que …	I think that …
J'ai l'impression …	I have the impression …
À mon avis …	In my opinion …

Going into the next semester, the bond between Aleksandra, Julie and myself became more intimate. The more we used *passé composé*, the more we revealed about ourselves and the things we did in our lives, and the more we discovered we had a lot in common.

Aleksandra had a taste for the small pleasures in life—a great film, a magnificent piece of cake. Whenever she would describe these kinds of experiences her eyes would widen with an obvious lust for life. And she loved to tell a good story.

'My class didn't show up on Saturday morning, so I went to the cafe … I was sitting, drinking coffee, reading *le journal* … Then I looked at my watch, *merde!* … I ran back to the Alliance but it was closed and there was a big lock on the car park gate. My 'usband came with some bolt-cutters and opened it. When I came to work I tried to sneak in but the director said, *Aleksaaaandra?* … I have to pay them back. Anyway, what did you do in the last week that was interesting?'

Every class began with the same question: what did you do in the last week that was interesting? It was the part of class we most enjoyed, and it was a very effective way to practice *passé composé*.

There was actually quite a bit going on in my life that I considered exciting. As gURLpool became better known, the publicity increased and the membership grew, and it was becoming easier to gather stories and be granted interviews. In fact, after a few months we began to be offered story ideas and interviews.

A couple of months after I started work, gURLpool hired two more journalists, which took some of the pressure off me in relation to the workload but also meant there were other people to share the constant scrutiny from Sarah. Maeve, an aging journalist who, according to her, had spent her whole life working for unreasonable bosses and being ripped off, was particularly highly strung and often locked horns with Sarah.

Maeve was one of the funniest people I had ever met. On her first day, Sarah took her around to everyone's desk and introduced them.

'This is Margie', Sarah began.

'Oh, I know Margie!' Maeve exclaimed with exaggeration. 'Baby, I *love* your work.' I laughed out loud, while Sarah stood there with a blank expression.

From the moment we met, Maeve and I became friends. She was *not* glamorous and she found the day-to-day parade of fashion and egos incredible. She was a smoker and we would sit out the front of the building smoking and laughing at the comings and goings of the magazine. Maeve was equally able to laugh at herself and she often took the piss out of how un-gURLpool she was. Yet, any criticism she received from Sarah wounded her. She could never really get a handle on the fact that Sarah was the editor and her boss. Not that she disliked Sarah. She just thought that with her years of experience, it should be her.

Maeve's arrival meant that I was able to just sit in peace and write more often. In Sarah's life, Maeve's hissy fits about the way Sarah spoke to us took priority over my odd typo. Although there were still times I was rattled.

One of the first big international interviews I was offered was with Jamie Oliver, the 'Naked Chef', whose television show and series of cookbooks were the current talk of the town. Oliver was in Australia on a whirlwind tour, and thanks to a friendship I had developed with the publicity agent of his publisher, I was one of the few journalists outside of the daily newspapers and television to be granted an interview.

Everyone at gURLpool was excited about the interview and felt it would raise the profile of the magazine. Sarah was happy for me and recounted the stories of her first interviews with international stars (although now that she was friendly with so many, it seemed like a million years ago). Yet, when I got on the phone with Oliver, Sarah took over.

'So how are you enjoying Australia?' I began by asking.

'Margie!' Sarah cried. 'You've only got five minutes, ask something interesting!'

For the next five minutes I tried to block out the sound of Sarah despairing, and focus on Oliver's answers. At one stage I had to turn around to face Liz, because I momentarily stammered when Sarah put her face in her hands and muttered something like 'Don't ask *that* ...'

In the end Sarah really liked the article I produced, although she said I needed to work on conveying the personality of the star more, rather than just the words they said in the interview. 'That,' she said, 'is what makes a great celebrity interviewer'.

Working at gURLpool was exhausting—long hours, strict deadlines, ego battles every day—but I didn't care because to me it was exciting. The people I was interviewing, the functions we were invited to, and the sassy style of writing we produced were exactly what I had dreamed of. Being on staff as a journalist was something completely different from the freelancing I had done in the past. I felt like I was part of creating something amazing and as every issue came out I felt an incredible sense of pride.

One of my favourite activities at gURLpool was going to the media screenings of movies. Not only did they mean we got to see films before they were released, we did so on work time. Sitting in tiny theatrettes with a handful of journalists was a treat, although I laughed to myself at how serious some reviewers tried to look with their clipboards and their pens with little lights attached.

In French class, Aleksandra and Julie would listen intently to my descriptions of the latest French film, which I was privileged to see before it was released in cinemas. The main thing that Julie, Aleksandra and I had in common was our love for French cinema. Aleksandra had seen so many French films that she knew all the actors and directors, and all the gossip as well. At the end of every class she would alert us to any French films that were showing on SBS and sometimes we would spend half an hour of the next class talking about them.

'On est allé … qu'est-ce que c'est go to the pub?' It was the fourth lesson of intermediate but it was the same question either Julie or I asked every week.

At the beginning of every class when Aleksandra asked everyone what we did in the past week, Julie and I would need to say we went to the pub and did our homework. Yet, every week we needed to be told how to say 'went to the pub' again.

It just wouldn't stick. We had discovered that there were expressions that stuck in your head, which you could wheel out without even thinking about them and others that, no matter how often you had the phrase repeated to you, you would never remember.

For us it was *prendre un pot*—to take a drink. We knew other people struggled with their own expressions; *faire du shopping* was a common one because that translated to 'do shopping', when in English the verb is simply 'to shop'. Yet the phrase for us was not particularly difficult to understand—just impossible to remember. *Prendre un pot*. It was very unfortunate because every weekend we were going to the pub.

After weeks of baffling forgetfulness, Julie and I decided to just write it down so we could read it in class. And also to use the phrase as often as we could. She would call me during the week. 'What day do you want to *prendre un pot* this weekend?' she would say.

Slowly it began to stick, although for some inexplicable reason, it never really felt comfortable. Aleksandra would snigger quietly when we used it and we always thought it was because she was remembering how difficult it had been for us to remember it.

Around a year later, when we were in the Advanced course, Julie used *prendre un pot* in a sentence. Our teacher at the time corrected it to *prendre un verre*, which literally translates to take a glass. 'Prendre un pot,' he explained, 'is an expression only used by peasants'.

'That little bitch!' Julie laughed on the way home, referring to Aleksandra. But we were quietly very impressed with her trick.

We spent much of our classes with Aleksandra laughing at ourselves. It made tolerable a fact that we were trying to deny—Julie and I were butchering the French language. Our grammar was gradually improving and by now we could use several tenses, although a lot of thought was required and often there were large pauses between our words and sentences. What was really humiliating, though, was our pronunciation.

At the beginning of every semester, when the new students are being forced to explain why they want to learn French, one of the common responses is, 'French is such a beautiful language'. And it is. It doesn't have the harshness of some of the Germanic languages and it sounds smoother than Asian languages. No matter what is being said, French sounds romantic and poetic. Just not the way we were speaking it.

We had spent so much time learning verb conjugations and sentence structure that our vocabulary had been neglected. We spent much time looking up the names of objects, places and things in the dictionary. Discovering the word you needed was one thing; learning to pronounce it was a different thing altogether.

One night in class, we were watching a short article on the French news about a tornado that had flattened some small towns in America. After we watched it, Aleksandra asked some questions, starting with 'what country is this?'

'Les États-Unis', I volunteered. Aleksandra burst out laughing. 'What?' I demanded. Aleksandra tried to tell me, but was unable to control her laughter. Soon everyone was laughing too, although they had no idea why.

I knew this word because I had read it in a French magazine. United States is les États-Unis. What was ridiculous was the way I pronounced it, 'lesetusoony'—elongated and with a slight twang. Actually, that is very close to the way it is pronounced—except at twice the speed, and with the emphasis on completely different syllables.

The French never elongate their words the way we do in Australia. Their words are formed by short, sharp sounds. This often leads to

French students complaining about the speed in which the French speak. The way I said *les États-Unis* was correct but was so drawn out. When spoken with a twang, Aleksandra told me, no French speaker would know what I had said.

After that episode, Julie and I made a conscious effort to not elongate our words, but it was difficult. It takes confidence that you have chosen the correct word and the correct pronunciation to blurt it out. It is a natural response to draw out a word if you are unsure.

Most of the time, though, Aleksandra knew what we were trying to say and would make us repeat the word until it was spoken correctly. Nonetheless, it reinforced to Julie and I that when we spoke French it was not a beautiful language. And it also brought back the feelings of embarrassment and humiliation I had felt as a child when I said the wrong thing.

In my family, speaking up could be very confusing. My mother, an intellectual and a woman with a keen interest in human rights and the women's movement, encouraged us from an early age to be interested in the world beyond our own community, and to develop our own opinions. While Mum encouraged us to speak our minds, Dad encouraged us to speak as little as possible, and when we did, it was simply to be charming. I learnt at an early age that what would make Dad smile was when I mispronounced a word or asked a silly question. If he laughed, it was a successful transaction of words. If it made guests laugh, it would be a real victory. 'It's a good thing Margie is so pretty!' Dad would say.

Although the feeling of embarrassment and shame was similar, when I did mispronounce a word or sentence in French class, I knew that laughing about it would remove at least some of the embarrassment. Aleksandra wasn't on a power trip, though, and she went to great pains to lessen the humiliation involved in speaking out loud. She said that for an Australian to speak French she must strop drawling. It also worked the other way for the French trying to speak in English.

'There are some words a French teacher will never say in English', she explained. 'Beach, *par exemple*.' It took a second before the class realised that if you don't draw out the 'ea' sound, the word would sound like 'bitch'.

The class chuckled. 'And we will always call this a 'andout', Aleksandra continued, picking up a piece of paper. The class didn't get it. 'Well', she smiled, 'I can 'ardly say I am going to pass around a shit.'

Chapter 10
A strange assortment of classmates

Apercevoir (to notice or realise)
Apercevoir qqn (to notice someone)
J'aperçois Jacques au milieu de la foule.
I see Jacques in the middle of the crowd.

S'apercevoir de + nom (to realise)
Il ne s'est pas aperçu de son erreur.
He didn't realise his error.

'Can you come up? I'm not quite ready', asked Julie. I was waiting in my car out the front of Julie's apartment building to pick her up for French, and after about ten minutes called her to hurry her up.

As I climbed the stairs I realised that although Julie and I had been friends for months I had never been to her home. I knew all about her work at the bank, her friends and her family, and we saw each other every weekend, which was more than I saw most of my other friends, but our relationship was all about French. We'd go to classes together, study together and see French films together. But we had never done anything that wasn't related to French.

Julie had opened the front door and I let myself in. As soon as I saw it I wished that I were single and living in an apartment. Julie's apartment was pure sixties glamour. The furniture was modern. There was a huge white sofa in the centre of the room and a large faux-fur rug on the floor.

On the feature wall hung an enormous reproduction of a poster for the French film *La Fille sur le Pont*, and stacked neatly on the coffee table were a pile of French magazines. On the lowboy that extended across one wall were Julie's CDs and DVDs—mostly bearing French titles.

My family often remarked that going to my house was like stepping into a scene from a French movie, but my house was nothing like this. Julie had gone for the bachelor in Paris mode of interior decorating, whilst my house was more the Moulin Rouge inspired abode. Where Julie had chosen funky designs and modern furniture, I had gone for heavy velvet curtains, oriental-inspired fittings, chandeliers and Moroccan influences.

Of course, Julie's circumstances were somewhat different from my own. I lived in a house with a large dog and a partner and she lived in an apartment by herself. Whilst my home was undoubtedly as *très* Parisian as Julie's, it required a certain amount of dusting, which, I thought enviously, Julie's probably did not.

I felt a sudden rush of affection for Julie. She was unashamedly a Francophile—right down to her interior decorating. Everything about her life had a French feel—the books she read, the music she listened to, the clothes she wore. Somehow, I had managed to befriend someone just like me. The only difference was, the more Parisian my house became, the more I felt slightly ashamed. Julie wasn't the slightest bit self-conscious about it.

I walked past the cocktail bar into the bedroom where Julie was putting the finishing touches on her look. In contrast to the living area, Julie's bedroom was a mess. The bed was unmade and there were clothes and shoes everywhere. The bathroom wasn't much better—every shelf was crammed with cosmetics and make-up.

Julie slipped on her red stilettos and stood up. 'Okay', she said. 'I'm ready.' Throughout the Beginners course, we had a new class every semester. Although everyone started out full of hope and optimism, Julie and I were the only students who ever continued on. On the first day of class we would meet a whole new batch of classmates that Julie and I referred to fondly as 'the freaks'; a motley crew of would-be Francophiles, bored housewives and office workers with dreams of speaking an exotic language.

Part Two: Intermediate

Our Intermediate class contained the usual mix of students but one of them was a rare example of someone who took French too seriously but actually stuck with it. Chris combined his desire to learn French with a relentless dedication which, put to better use, could convert bin Laden to Judaism.

Chris turned up to every class ten minutes late and out of breath. He was a slightly balding, self-employed insurance salesman who worked out of an office in the eastern suburbs. He was in his early forties, had never been married and had no children. Chris was Greek, and although he never said so, Julie and I surmised that he was living at home. Such was his sheer determination that Julie and I concluded that someone must have told him to 'get a life', a remark that had prompted a bit of soul-searching and the obvious conclusion drawn by many middle-aged Greek boys with no life—adult education.

Chris wasn't just learning French; he was also studying Italian and Greek (the way the language was meant to be spoken, not the way his mama spoke it at home). Every Thursday Chris would turn up and unpack his satchel: three identical purple folders (in mint condition), with white labels on the top right corner, which simply read, 'Greek', 'French' and 'Italian'. The folders would be followed by the crisp, white notepad, a pen (for writing notes on the pad) and a pencil (for writing notes in the textbook). Once unpacked, Chris would sigh, clasp his hands together and smile at Aleksandra as if to say, 'I'm here, I'm ready, you may start'.

Sometimes it seemed that Chris was more interested in having learnt a language than he was in actually learning it. He was forever marking his progress by how far the class progressed through the textbook, *Tempo*. God help us if the class should get through only two pages of the book, instead of three, which was standard. 'Should we do the next page for *devoirs maison* so we don't fall behind?' he would ask Aleksandra, his obvious distress thinly masked by a panicked smile.

There was nothing offensive about Chris; he was always pleasant and charming, but as a student he was just about the most annoying person I had ever met. He would frequently drown out the responses of other students with his own loud, booming voice. Whenever he would be corrected he would need to know exactly how he was wrong and be allowed to make up some of his own examples, just to make sure he really did understand his error and wouldn't be repeating it. The time it took and the uselessness for the rest of the class didn't matter. It was all about Chris and his quest to becoming multilingual. Often Aleksandra would ask a question and purposely avoid eye contact with Chris just so she wouldn't have to deal with him.

Chris saw himself as a linguist in the making. This wasn't a hobby for him; it was how he defined himself. The down side to his obsessive behaviour was that every time he made an error that might cause other class members to chuckle, he was mortally wounded. 'Oh, you said, *arrête*', he would exclaim a little too loudly. 'I thought you said *achète* because you were mumbling.' Chris would follow statements like this with a pleading smile to other class members. You could almost read his mind, 'Please don't think I made a silly mistake'.

At moments like this, it was hard not to feel sorry for Chris. Julie and I had long ago accepted that humiliation was part of the deal, and when we were in a similar situation we'd be embarrassed, for sure, but we'd laugh at ourselves in the car on the way home and eventually the incident would become part of our friendship folklore.

On one occasion though, Chris's attempt to keep up appearances turned nasty. French students were required to purchase two books— *Tempo*, that we worked through in the class and the *Tempo* exercise book that contained exercises for each corresponding chapter. *Tempo* had exercises also, but most of these were oral or listening exercises that we would do in class. Usually, *devoirs maison*, or homework, consisted of set exercises in the exercise book, but occasionally we would also need to complete exercises in *Tempo*. In those instances, the class would go over the answers in the following lesson. There was no need to go over the answers in the exercise book, because they were provided in the back of the book.

Towards the end of Beginners 4, we started the class by going through the homework from *Tempo*. Then Aleksandra commenced the class. 'Wait!' exclaimed Chris. 'What about the other homework? We haven't gone through that.' Julie and I looked at each other and rolled our eyes. It was the same scenario as almost every class. Chris would express his desire to go over the exercises and Aleksandra would tell him that there is no need because the answers are in the back of the book.

Of course, she would say it in French. And Chris would smile and nod that he understood and we'd move on. The problem for Chris was that he didn't actually understand what Aleksandra was saying. So great was his desire not to look like a fool, he just pretended that he understood, because obviously everyone else in the class did. So at the beginning of every class he would work himself into a lather, believing that there was work we had all forgotten to correct.

On this particular day Julie and I had had enough. 'Chris!' I exclaimed in English. 'The answers are in the back of the book!' At this, everyone began to chuckle, which added to his humiliation. He turned bright red and looked at Aleksandra. 'Yes, it's true,' she said, also in English, 'the answers are in the back of the book'.

Chris turned from red to purple and looked like the top of his head was about to explode. 'Well, why didn't you tell me that then?' he hissed at Aleksandra. Although Aleksandra appeared unfazed and continued with the class, we were all shocked at seeing the dark side of Chris and the way he had treated Aleksandra. We were all subdued for the rest of the class. Chris, on the other hand, was overly cheerful and friendly. We assumed it was his attempt to restore his image that he had temporarily let lapse.

The *passé composé* not only allowed us to become better acquainted with how our teacher spent her week, but also how the other members of the class spent theirs. And learning the *subjonctif* revealed their hopes and desires. Until now, Julie was the only friendship I had made through French classes. Talking about ourselves revealed the personalities of the people we wouldn't normally talk to, and opened us up to the reasons why such an unlikely group of people were learning French.

Our first impressions of Bag Lady may have been marred by the fact that we found her physically off-putting. If she hadn't told us in her introduction that she was a computer technician, we would have guessed she was homeless. Bag Lady was obese and had long, lank, grey hair that was permanently greasy. A long fringe made her scrunched up face appear more so, and she wore thick glasses and a constant frown.

She never seemed to have a good word to say about anything. If we were talking about a movie that had been on TV she would grunt and say she doesn't watch TV because it's too commercial. When Aleksandra asked her what she did during the week she would groan and say she had to work because everyone in her office was incompetent and left everything for her to do.

Over time, Julie and I came to realise that Bag Lady was actually trying to cultivate her unappealing look. She wanted to look downtrodden and miserable, because she wanted us to think she was an intellectual, discouraged with the state of the world.

Chances are she really was discontented with the human race, but we did have occasion to believe she was looking for any excuse to tell us all about how much more intellectual than us she was. Aleksandra once asked her why she was studying French and her response was to moan and mumble, 'I have to leave Australia. I can't stand the way the government is treating the refugees ...'

I'm sure she was hoping we'd all be nodding seriously and thinking what a socially conscious intellect this woman was, but we were really thinking, what the hell is she talking about? She wants to leave Australia because of the refugee crisis and then what? Move to France, a country with an appalling, imperialist attitude and culture that prides itself on racism? A country with a disgraceful human rights record, where it's socially acceptable to discriminate against blacks?

At the end of one of our lessons, Bag Lady, Julie and I walked to our cars together and she made a scoffing comment about how she hoped one of the other girls wouldn't continue because, 'She's so hopeless, she'll end up holding the rest of us back'. That comment caused momentary panic in Julie and me because we were both thinking that she would make life difficult for us if we, too, weren't up to her standards.

Part Two: Intermediate

Despite Bag Lady's appearance, she ended up being one of the few students Julie and I encountered who we actually looked forward to seeing. Some semesters later, when we discovered we had a new teacher, Bag Lady said to us, 'I'm sad that the foursome has broken up'. It took a while for Julie and I to work out what she meant, but then we realised she meant Aleksandra, Julie, herself and me. We were touched.

Bag Lady saw the tenderness and friendship between me, Julie and Aleksandra and she wanted to be part of it. She made a point of being friendly, sympathetic and even like-minded when the occasion called for it. Over time, she began watching French movies and discussing them with the rest of us. She would smile and laugh and tell us if she had seen a Daniel Auteuil movie, knowing he was our favourite actor.

During the last class of Intermediate 4, conversation turned to babies. Bag Lady and Aleksandra were having a conversation although I wasn't paying too much attention. Suddenly, I realised that Bag Lady was talking about her own baby. I don't know why it never occurred to us that she would have a family, but we were shocked. Bag Lady stopped being a grotty, overweight object of our amusement and became a worn-out woman who worked ridiculously long hours and had a new baby and a young child at home. For Bag Lady, our weekly French lessons were the only time in her life she did something just for herself.

While Bag Lady's attitude became more positive over time, every so often she'd slip back into pessimism. She was miserable going into Intermediate 5 without Aleksandra as our teacher so Julie and I tried to put a positive spin on it for her. 'Claire seems really nice', we said encouragingly after the first class. 'I think she'd be better suited to modelling than teaching', Bag Lady muttered before hunching her shoulders and heading back to her car.

Other people in the class remained a mystery to us. Why Olivier was learning French was anyone's guess—even by Intermediate standards he was fluent and had an excellent accent. He arrived at the beginning of Intermediate 4 and left at the end of semester. If we were in high school, he'd have been the mysterious newcomer who broke all the girls' hearts. He was dark and handsome and had a laidback, Clarke Gable aura.

How much effort he put into studying, and how much he wanted to learn French were also a mystery. He simply turned up to class, answered the questions, wrote notes and went home. And after that one semester, Olivier never returned to the Alliance.

A few months after he left, I was sitting in my car at the traffic lights in Fitzroy Street when I noticed a man looking at me. In no mood for idiots, I wound down my window and demanded, 'Do I *know* you?'

'Actually, you do', he said without expression and boarded his tram. Practically every waking thought my mind produced over the next twenty-four hours was devoted to trying to figure out who this man was. Then I realised it was Olivier.

Towards the end of the semester Chris was becoming increasingly frustrated with the French classes—or more particularly, at the rate of his learning. One night, Julie and I were hurriedly trying to finish our homework exercises before Aleksandra arrived. Chris proudly announced that he had never not completed his homework. 'I devote every Saturday to studying French,' he boasted. 'I don't go out, I don't answer the phone, I just do exercises, practice my writing, do verb drills. You girls should do that.'

'Except that we have lives', Julie mumbled under her breath.

The success of his work was not really apparent. Chris continued to speak with a horrible Australian accent and still had difficulty understanding what was being said in class, but we did admire his dedication. It was no surprise to us when, at the end of the last class, Chris announced that he was not coming back. He had decided to switch to Saturday morning classes. 'They are four hours long', he said happily. 'That means I'll know French twice as fast!'

Chapter 11

Margie exaggerates her ability to speak French to interview a star

Speaking on the telephone

Bonjour. Je voudrais parler à qqn ... s'il vous plaît.
Hello. I would like to speak to ... please.
C'est de la part de qui?
Who is calling?
Il n'est pas ici pour le moment.
He is not here at the moment.
Est-ce que je pourrais lui laisser un message?
Am I able to leave him a message?
Bien sûr. Je vais le prendre.
Of course. Let me write it down.
Je rappellerai plus tard.
I will call back later.

'I speak French.' It seemed like a harmless comment at the time and I was fairly sure I wouldn't be called upon to actually do it, but I was wrong.

Every year, Palace Cinemas in Melbourne hosts the French film festival. It's a very popular event and not just with expats and Francophiles. Australia is the highest consumer of French cinema outside French-speaking nations, so French film distributors clamber to preview their offerings at the festival in the hope that the public reaction is so great, a distributor in Australia will pick it up.

For two weeks of the year, the Cinema Como in the exclusive suburb of South Yarra is transformed into a Francophile's dream. French flags are draped from the ceilings and walls; popcorn and Coke give way to cheese selections and fine wine and the foyer buzzes with the heated and expressive sounds of the French language.

The first year, Julie and I walked into the Como centre and our jaws dropped. Julie walked around gently touching the flags and displays like they were priceless antiques, and for some reason we started talking in hushed tones.

We picked up a program and ran through the synopses, circling the films we wanted to see. Normally, French films tend to fall into two categories, ultra-arthouse or ultra-commercial, but during the French film festival patrons can experience a wide range of cinematic offerings. When we had made our selection, we realised we would be seeing twelve films in just one week.

Perhaps we just got caught up in the moment, but after we'd actually sat through twelve films and were still happy to see more, we decided that our philosophy would be that there is no such thing as too much French cinema! And it's a philosophy that continues to this day. If a film looks even remotely interesting, we'll give it a go. Seeing two or three films in one day is not uncommon.

The most exceptional patisserie in Melbourne, Laurent, is situated in the Como complex. Between screenings Julie and I went to Laurent, sipped coffee, ate pastries and excitedly dissected the film we had just seen. It was the break from the ordinary that we loved. While French cinema has a reputation for being dark, meaningless and full of nudity, there are a great number of French films that are highly intelligent and quirky, and increasingly aware of their growing international potential.

Given the popularity of the French film festival in Australia, some distributors, having snapped up the rights to a film, will ride the wave and immediately follow the festival with a lot of press. I had seen *Le Goût des Autres (The Taste of Others),* so when the film distributors contacted me and said that the director and star, Agnès Jaoui, was giving interviews, I immediately put my hand up. And, thinking it might increase my chances of success, I emailed the words, 'I speak French'.

I hadn't been particularly impressed with *Le Goût des Autres*, but I certainly didn't hate it. To me the film was very traditional, with struggling actors on the point of despair, lots of sex and no real resolution. I was eager to interview Jaoui because she is a celebrated actress in France and I had seen several of her films. Also, I figured that if I could write an impressive article it might open the door to interviews with other French actors.

Julie shrieked when I told her I was interviewing Agnès Jaoui. I was so excited that for a moment I dropped my professional veneer and shrieked too. Journalists try to never look impressed by the celebrities who they interview. Most entertainment journalists are also fans, but in their eyes, their profession allows them to keep at least some of their dignity. Julie thought it was just wonderful and I was buoyed by her enthusiasm. Hell, it *is* so cool, I thought to myself smugly.

The date and time for the interview were set up. I would get a call from France at a certain time and Jaoui would be on the line. A translator would be on a second line. Jaoui, it was explained to me, spoke English reasonably well and the translator was there just in case she got into trouble.

On the night in question I took the phone into my bedroom, attached the bug to the receiver and waited. Even though it was ten minutes after the scheduled time I wasn't worried because I knew she was doing back-to-back interviews and could easily run over time. Twenty minutes later the phone rang. It was the publicist, ringing to apologise. The interviews were running overtime and would I mind waiting about ten more minutes?

Not a problem, I said, although the nerves were killing me. Ten minutes later the phone rang, although it wasn't Jaoui, it was the publicist again. 'I am so sorry to do this to you,' she apologised, 'Agnès has become very upset'.

'What happened?' I asked.

'A reporter from a newspaper just gave her a hard time. He became a bit nasty about her poor English and so I told her to have a break for half an hour. Do you mind if we put off the interview until then?'

'Not at all', I said. I knew precisely how awful it was when you tried to understand what someone was saying and then got yelled at when you didn't. I was remembering the treatment I received from some of the French people and from my friends when we were in Paris for Millennium Eve.

'That's great, thank you Margie', said the publicist. 'It's so good that you are the next interview. Agnès will be so relieved to be able to speak in French.'

I almost dropped the phone in horror. Conduct the interview in French; she had to be kidding! Sure, I was in Intermediate 4, but there was no way I would be able to have an entire conversation in French! It would be all right if she submitted her answers to me in writing and in French. That way I would know exactly what words she was using, and could look up words I didn't understand. But listening to French was a completely different deal. All the words running into each other and at a rapid speed, film and acting vocabulary I had never heard before—I didn't stand a chance!

I hung up, my mind racing, desperately searching for a solution. Okay, I thought, I have the bug on the phone so it doesn't really matter what she says, I can try to translate it later. I could even take it to class and get Aleksandra to help me translate. My immediate problem was working out what I was going to say to her.

In the half-hour, I quickly scribbled down some questions in French. I resigned myself to the fact that it would be a pretty basic interview: How did you find directing and acting in the same film? What themes are in the film? Who are your favourite actors and why? At this stage, I didn't really care how shallow the questions were; I just wanted to get through it. My greatest fear was that she might ask *me* questions.

'Hello, is that Margaret?' a heavily accented voice asked when I picked up the phone. Thank God, I thought, she's speaking in English. Jaoui didn't sound rattled or upset, but just to make sure, I asked, 'Are you going to be okay if we do this interview in English?'

'Yes,' she assured me, 'but you must speak slowly'.

Part Two: Intermediate

I could have wept with relief. In fact, Jaoui's English was pretty good. I spoke slowly and simply and she answered with what I suspected were rehearsed responses. We discussed what it was like to write, direct and star in a film and her relationship with co-author and co-star, Jean Pierre Bacri. Occasionally she struggled with a word, but after prompting she got there.

I was more relaxed and was actually starting to enjoy listening to her. Then I turned the conversation to her character. 'How much are you like your character?' I asked. There was silence on the other end before Jaoui answered in a cool voice. 'What are you saying? That I sleep with a lot of men?'

Just as I went to protest, another voice entered the conversation, speaking forcefully and rapidly and giving me a terrible fright. It was the translator, who I hadn't realised was on a third line until that moment. Jaoui and the translator continued the heated conversation for about a minute, although it felt like hours, with me feebly interjecting, 'I didn't mean it like that ...'

'I am sorry about that,' said the translator sweetly, as though she were a completely different character, 'she didn't understand the question properly, but now she does'.

Jaoui answered the question, but the tone of the conversation had turned decidedly sour. Thankfully, the time was nearly up, and after one more question I thanked her politely and wished her well with the film. When I hung up I was covered in sweat. Agnès Jaoui wasn't the only one who was on the verge of a nervous breakdown.

★★★★

Julie and I both had huge crushes on the French actor Daniel Auteuil, something which many people had trouble understanding because he is not traditionally handsome. He's thinnish, has a large nose and eyes that look like they belong on a pigeon.

Julie fell in love with his passion and hopelessness in *The Girl on the Bridge*. In the film, Auteuil plays a washed-up knife thrower whose career is reignited when he falls desperately in love with his model at whom the knives are thrown. To Julie, Auteuil's character represented everything she believed true love to be—passion for which one would die, desperation and an unquestioning belief that the union was meant to be. The fact the character was French only added to the illusion. In her eyes, falling in love with a French man would be a romance of a lifetime.

For someone who was holding out for the great French lover, Julie spent a lot of time dating very ordinary men. She never spoke much about the men she dated, partly I think because she was embarrassed that her lapses in judgment might tarnish her glamorous French image, but occasionally she would relate stories about one man in particular who treated her pretty shabbily. He would only call her when he felt like it—or more accurately, when he felt like sex—would frequently stand her up and was often nasty in his comments about her. She would swear she was going to dump him, but every so often his name would come up when she was relating a story, so I knew she was still seeing him, even if it was on and off.

Yet, when Julie talked about her life plan—becoming a famous fashion journalist, attending parties and mixing with celebrities, having a residence in Paris—I never heard this guy's name mentioned. The name that frequently came up though, was Daniel Auteuil.

Even without Julie's notions of perfect love and romance, Daniel Auteuil has, without question, a certain *je ne sais quoi*. For me, he was attractive in *The Girl on the Bridge*, but he sealed the deal in sexiness as the captain in *The Widow of Saint Pierre*.

At the most recent film festival, Auteuil was in two films, *Sade* and *Le Placard*. The first film we saw was *Sade*, about the Marquis de Sade, who was a pioneering pornographer and wrote stories with violent and nasty themes. In fact, the word 'sadism' is derived from his name. Sade led a pretty rotten life. He was ostracised, jailed and he ended up without money or his family. *Sade* dealt with the period in his life in which he was imprisoned.

Interestingly, around the same time a film was made called *Quills*. It starred the Australian actor Geoffrey Rush as the Marquis de Sade and also dealt with a period in his life in which he was imprisoned. I had seen it and thought it was generally a bit of fluff, showing the Marquis as a wacky, harmless eccentric.

Sade was completely the opposite. Auteuil portrayed the Marquis as sleazy, predatory and a little bit sick, which was kind of sexy, yet a little disturbing. More real-life in other words. In particular, there is one scene in a barn in which Auteuil's character whips himself and then has sex with an under-age girl. It is graphic and even shows close-up digital penetration. For months afterwards Julie and I would say 'the barn' with a snigger.

Not surprisingly, *Le Placard* was picked up for general release not long after the film festival. We had loved *Le Placard* and not just because it starred Daniel Auteuil. From the opening scene we hadn't stopped laughing. Auteuil plays a boring, nerdy, middle-management accountant who works in a condom factory and accidentally discovers he's about to be retrenched. Having worked all his life in the one job and being happy with the routine of his life, he's thrown into turmoil. Egged on by his old gay neighbour he decides to pretend that he is homosexual—in the belief that a condom factory couldn't risk alienating members of the gay community if it was ever revealed that they had sacked a worker because he was gay.

It's a comedy of errors, which satirises political correctness and it's very clever. I knew that it had been picked up by Global films and more than anything I wanted to get an interview with Daniel Auteuil.

gURLpool had never worked with Global films—I had never even heard of them—and I think their public relations company was a one or two-woman operation. One of those women, Erika Brown, was the only thing standing between me and Daniel Auteuil.

To say she was cautious is an understatement. When I called, she was very reluctant to give gURLpool passes to give away in a promotion, let alone grant interviews.

'Please don't take this the wrong way,' she said when I called, 'but I just don't know your magazine and I need to know that whoever is going to do the interview is a professional'. She sounded as though she was in her early forties and wasn't really comfortable playing the PR game.

'I understand', I said patiently. 'We're the largest online magazine in Australia and just like every magazine and newspaper, we do employ professional journalists and editors.'

'Hmm, I'm sure you are right. I just don't know if he wants to give interviews. Tell me again how giveaways work?'

I went through my proposal, although what I really wanted to say was, 'What is wrong with you? Don't you realise that I am offering coverage of this movie that equals thousands of dollars in advertising and an endorsement that would be hard to put a price on?'

'I tell you what,' she said at one stage, 'if you do a promotion for *Le Placard*, I'll send you an invitation to the media screening'.

She had to be kidding. Distribution companies send out invitations to media screenings as a matter of course. They are worth nothing to them—it costs nothing to screen a film and reviewers have to see a film in order to review it. They are certainly not viewed by anyone as a perk.

I think, in part, she was enjoying listening to me rave about her film and the power she now had. But it was driving me crazy. I think she had been given the rights to a film that distributors thought would perform okay in cinemas, but which turned out to be a blockbuster—and she just couldn't handle it.

Meanwhile, our French class was following with interest the saga of emails and phone calls in the attempt to get Daniel Auteuil. Aleksandra was beside herself with the prospect that I may be able to speak with our hero. Even those people who had never seen Daniel Auteuil in a movie were fascinated with all the political wheelings and dealings.

Finally, I had to admit defeat. Erika was still dragging her feet, trying to get more and more out of us and I was beginning to doubt whether she actually had the power to organise an interview anyway. I explained to the class about my last-ditch attempt.

'So I sent her a basket with cheeses, biscuits and chocolates.'

'Ooh la la!' exclaimed Aleksandra. 'What did she say?'

'She said Daniel Auteuil doesn't like to speak English. I just can't understand. I am offering free publicity. Doesn't he want to promote his film?'

'No, he would not care.' Aleksandra shrugged. 'He has made the film. He has been paid. It is more the film company that would want to promote the film.'

'I guess so', I agreed. 'Anyway, she said he was doing one interview only and she was going to give it to *The Australian* because it has a lot of readers.'

Aleksandra had pondered the Daniel Auteuil situation for a moment. 'This is what you should do,' she had said triumphantly at last, 'send him a photograph of yourself'.

I laughed with good humour, but she was deadly serious. 'He will speak to a beautiful girl, of course', she said definitively. 'That is the way we do things in France.'

Julie was in hysterics. She couldn't believe that in the end I resorted to outright bribery. 'And it was so funny hearing you talk about Daniel in French to Aleksandra!' she laughed on the way home. We still found it hysterical that we were beginning to be able to explain and recount events in French. It may have said 'Intermediate' on the door, but we still felt like absolute beginners.

As much as I wanted an interview with Daniel Auteuil, I didn't send him a photo of myself. The decision had nothing to do with professional integrity, or a belief that I was an intelligent, talented journalist, not just a pretty face. I was just mortified at the thought of it ever getting out in media circles that I was sending movie stars photos of myself. It may be what they did in France, but I was in Australia. The experience wasn't a total write-off, I thought. At least now I was known to Global, and this would not be the last film that Daniel Auteuil would make. In the meantime, I could work on making my French perfect.

Chapter 12
Julie gets tough

Time

une heure: à huit heures	a time: at eight o'clock
un jour: le 14 février	a day: 14 February
un mois: en juin	a month: in June
une année: en 1806	a year: in 1806

When Julie and I arrived for the first lesson of Intermediate 5, we were horrified to discover that the teacher standing at the board was not Aleksandra, but a lanky, nerdy man in his mid-twenties who introduced himself as Marc.

Julie and I had secretly worried that Aleksandra may not be coming back, because at the end of the previous semester she brought a camera to class and had taken our photo. Yet, we had assured each other that it might just mean that she had leftover film on a roll. Now it seemed obvious that we had been kidding ourselves.

A teacher change is particularly stressful for students. Technically, your ear becomes accustomed to the accent, tone and rate of speech of a teacher, so it can actually be quite difficult to understand another teacher. There's also comfort in the familiarity of their teaching methods. We knew that Aleksandra would begin every class by asking us if we had done anything interesting during the week, and engage us in conversation about what that was in order to practice our past tenses. We also knew that Aleksandra was a film buff and could talk for ages about actors and movies. There were no surprises with Aleksandra. And there are trust issues. We knew that Aleksandra was harmless; she wouldn't hound us like Xamuel or humiliate us when we became lost. Aleksandra liked us and we liked her.

But there we were in a room full of strangers. Julie had never had a teacher change before and was looking particularly anxious. The first thing that struck us about Marc was that he spoke in English the entire time. While that was, admittedly, a relief, we couldn't help feeling a little ripped off. Sure, it was an easy ride, but you don't get on the Big Dipper if you want a merry-go-round ride. Our doubts about Marc were confirmed when he introduced himself and announced that he was teaching at the Alliance because he wanted to improve his English.

During the class he asked us what the English word for something was rather than us asking for the French. Julie and I scribbled notes to each other, which amounted to, 'I hate Marc!'

There have been two times during the course of our studies when Julie and I have exchanged The Look. The Look is an expression that encompasses terror and non-comprehension at the same time. Of course, there have been times when we've been terrified and these are normally the times we haven't understood something and it seems like the whole class is waiting for us to say something. That happens fairly regularly. The two experiences that have prompted The Look have been different. The terror part is just straight fear, but the non-comprehension bit is not a lack of understanding the language, but of not understanding what is going on around us.

Julie was the first of us to wear The Look and it happened in Marc's class. So disturbing was the experience that when it seemed like it might happen again she nearly burst into tears. It started when we introduced ourselves. All the others had done it by the time we arrived, so Julie and I were the only ones left. I started: *'Je m'appelle Margie. Je suis journaliste, et j'habite à Elwood avec mon mari et mon chien. J'adore le film français.'*

Everyone nodded and smiled politely. Someone asked me who I worked for and when I responded they all continued to nod and smile. Then it was Julie's turn. *'Je m'appelle Julie'*, she said. *'J'habite à Elwood aussi. J'adore le film français aussi …'*

I honestly cannot explain what happened next, and God knows Julie and I have discussed it at length. Suddenly and without warning, all those nodding, smiling people turned into interrogation officers, firing off question after question at Julie.

'What films do you like?' 'Who is your favourite actor?' Then the questions got specific. 'When did you last see a French film?' 'Are you going to see a film on the weekend?'

It was like Julie had done something wrong and was being hounded into a confession. She sat there with The Look on her face; her smile plastered in position, but eyes that showed pure terror, answering the questions very slowly, as if giving herself time to figure out what was going on. But she never did. Eventually Marc interrupted because he wanted the class to begin.

The class turned their attention away from Julie and smiled at Marc. The experience was bizarre but it really rattled Julie. During the class, one of the students was describing what someone looked like. Marc turned to the room and said the word '*ensemble*'. Then he asked, 'What do you call an *ensemble*—like a skirt, shirt and jacket—in English?' Everyone thought about it for a second. Then he turned to Julie. 'Well?' he asked.

'Ensemble', Julie answered.

'No', replied Marc. 'What do you call it in English?'

'An ensemble', she hissed between gritted teeth.

'No!' Marc insisted. 'In English!'

By this stage Julie was red with rage and close to tears. 'It's the same as in English!' she yelled.

'Or you could call it an outfit', someone else in the class offered, feebly.

That was it for Julie; Marc was the enemy. Not only was he not Aleksandra, he was a moron who didn't understand what an ensemble was. The next week when we arrived at class, Julie walked into the room before me and her face lit up with pure joy. 'Aleksandra's back!' she exclaimed. I thought she was going to run up and give her a hug. She didn't, but Aleksandra looked particularly chuffed for the rest of the class. Aleksandra explained that she had been in France visiting her family. 'I showed them the photograph I took of you in the last class.' She smiled. 'And they all said, I have a beautiful class.' It was no wonder we loved Aleksandra.

Julie and I were always the youngest in every class we passed through. It added a nice balance to the class because we contributed humour and liveliness to what would be an otherwise stressful situation for the older members of the class. Chris and the other woman left after Intermediate 2, to study on Saturday mornings, and when we turned up to the first class of Intermediate 3, we discovered that there were only the four of us: Julie, myself, Bag Lady and a brand new freak, Brendan. A younger freak.

Brendan was a nerd, but a friendly one. He was in his early twenties, freckly, skinny, and dressed very sensibly for the cold evenings in perfectly ironed jeans, with shirts and jumpers. He studied mathematics and science during the day and was clearly very intelligent. He had studied French at high school and although he wasn't pursuing languages as part of his tertiary education, he wanted to build on the skills he already had. He was that type of guy.

The one thing I will always remember about Brendan was how much he enjoyed the French classes. I'm sure that at no other time in his uni day would Brendan get to sit and chat to a handful of glamorous older women and he always had a smile on his face. He didn't stress one little bit about the lessons; he was just happy to be part of the group.

One evening one of the exercises we had to do involved describing a book that we had read recently and explaining why we liked it. I spoke about *Captain Corelli's Mandolin*, which had recently been made into a film and Julie talked about a biography she was reading about Vanessa Paradis. Brendan started talking about his book and Aleksandra appeared really interested. I couldn't work out what he was talking about.

We must have had baffled expressions on our faces, because he turned to us and said in English, 'It's the biography of the man who invented petrol'. Our baffled expressions must have changed to disbelief because he added, laughing, 'It really is interesting'.

Brendan had such a great attitude that Julie and I really warmed to him. Having said that, I really can't explain why I did such a mean thing to him. After the second last class Brendan walked me to my car. Julie was away that night, and Brendan and I were chatting about how the semester was drawing to an end. 'Do you guys usually do anything on the last day of class?' he asked.

'Yes,' I said, 'we all make a plate of French food and bring it to class and have a party'. As soon as I said it I knew it was evil, but I couldn't help myself. In the car on the way home I figured the way I could undo this meanness would be for Julie and I to both bring a plate of something the following week and we really would have a party. The only problem with the plan was that I had forgotten all about it by the time I arrived home.

I remembered about an hour before the following class. I didn't know what to do, so I quickly texted Julie and confessed to my crime. 'That is so funny', she wrote back. 'Why don't we say we were going to bring something but ran out of time?'

That sounded like a good solution; like we were really planning a party but unfortunately weren't able to bring our plates of food. We arrived at class and sure enough, there was Brendan with a plate full of pastries he had bought from an authentic French bakery. Julie couldn't help herself and burst into fits of laughter. It only took a few seconds for Aleksandra and Brendan to realise what had happened.

'I think I have been the victim of a practical joke', Brendan explained to Aleksandra.

'I am so, so sorry!' I spluttered. 'I really was meaning to bring something, but I forgot!' Aleksandra shook her head and waved her finger at me, saying something I didn't catch but imaged was to the effect of, 'You bad, bad person'.

I was mortified. What if Aleksandra didn't like me anymore? What if our great relationship was over? Then Aleksandra turned to write something on the board and I noticed that her shoulders were moving in a suppressed chuckle.

Chapter 13
Julie wangles a trip to France

At the theatre

Je veux aller au théâtre.
I want to go to the theatre.
Y a-t-il un guide des spectacles?
Is there a theatre guide?
Je voudrais réserver deux places.
I'd like to book two tickets.
Quel genre de spectacle voudrais-tu voir?
What type of play would you like to see?

The distributors had high hopes for the new French film *Va Savoir*. *Amélie* had recently been an enormous commercial success in Australia, and the distributors were hoping that *Va Savoir*, also a quirky romantic comedy, would follow in its footsteps.

Va Savoir looked like a French version of *Friends* and follows three beautiful men and three beautiful women as their lives become entangled during the run of a play in Paris. The star of *Va Savoir*, Hélène de Fougerolles, had spent ten years doing cinema and she was a familiar face in the photo coverage of the Cannes Film Festival every year. She was fast becoming one of the most recognised faces in French cinema, but outside France she was probably best known for her role in the Leonardo DiCaprio blockbuster, *The Beach*. She was cute and sweet—and she was giving interviews.

Although naturally I had a keen interest in interviewing French actors, my doing so wasn't entirely self-serving. Ben, the technical guy at gURLpool, had developed a system that enabled us to track how many reads individual articles were getting. And reviews of French films were being very well read.

The French film festival had been officially opened by Jean-Philippe Bottin, the director of the Alliance Française, who said in his speech that the film festival was very important to the French film industry because Australia is the biggest consumer of French films outside their country of origin. The statistics on gURLpool supported this. There were either a lot of Francophiles or a lot of film buffs in Australia.

Palace Cinemas had apparently liked the piece I wrote about Agnès Jaoui and offered me the chance to interview Hélène de Fougerolles. It was the same-set up as before. At a designated time I would get the call, only this time there would be no translator. Hélène de Fougerolles spoke perfect English.

'You've worked with some great actors of French cinema—Daniel Auteuil and Isabelle Adjani', I started excitedly. 'How does that feel?'

'Always, it's about the movie, it's about the director—it's not really about who is my partner', de Fougerolles answered seriously. Then almost immediately the facade dropped and she broke into giggles. 'Although, often you don't even come to know them. In *La Reine Margot* I was an extra and I didn't meet the actors, I only looked at them. I didn't come to Daniel Auteuil and say, how are you today?'

I laughed at the thought of a stranger marching right up to Auteuil and asking 'How are you today?' and because Hélène de Fougerolles was so refreshingly honest. She was clearly star-struck with certain big-name actors, some of whom she had worked with, and there was absolutely no evidence of the overly large ego I had come to expect from most actors.

'You've done twenty-two movies in your career', I continued. 'That's so many for someone so young!'

'The first movies I have done, sometimes it was only for maybe three days or four days—it's only the last five years I have done big characters in movies.'

'Are you finding working in the film industry easier now that you are becoming better known?'

'It's always very stressful when you start a movie—the first day is awful. I don't eat. I don't sleep. And castings! I have already done so many castings in the ten years I have been in the industry. I thought it would get easier but it just gets worse and worse. That's because these days when I do a casting it's because I want to do the movie and it is very important for me to get it. The castings that I have done before were for anything—for commercials, for television, for anything. Today it's for something I really want to do.'

At the time, the film title on the lips of the worldwide cinema-going public was *Amélie*, which had signalled a turning point in French films. It was very commercial and followed a Hollywood formula, and while it opened the eyes of regular cinemagoers to French film, there were some traditionalists worried that French cinema was in danger of becoming too commercial and too American. When I asked de Fougerolles about this, she explained, 'The good thing is that before— like ten years ago—we were doing only one type of movie. The French public all wanted to see American movies, they didn't want to see a French movie. Now, *Amélie* is so popular, and that's good because now we can do popular things and we can do independent things. It's very nice here in France to have both.'

The *tournage* (shooting) of *Va Savoir*, de Fougerolles explained, was extraordinary. The script was written as the film was being made and every day the actors would be presented with the day's script, making it almost impossible for them to 'get into' character.

'I asked Jacques, what is Do like? How do you want her to be? And he was like, "she is just like what you are". So she is pretty much like me. I didn't work a lot on the character because I did not have a script, and I didn't know what would be the evolution of the character.'

And that was one thing I was learning about interviewing French actors—they're surprisingly honest. It made a refreshing change from the tired, rehearsed answers that journalists get from American and even Australian celebrities.

★★★★

Julie had always been extremely committed to our French classes—they were an essential part of our desire to become French—but at this year's film festival, and in our classes, she was more fired up than ever. She was going to France.

Well, actually she was going to London. The bank was sending Julie's supervisor to a five-day conference in London and she had decided to take Julie, her assistant. Although Julie wasn't thrilled about having to work, she had managed to extend her trip by two days, so she could spend the weekend in France.

Julie's father had mentioned his daughter's business trip to one of his clients, who was French. The client had told his family, who lived in the south-west city of Toulouse, and they had written to Julie, asking her to come and stay with them. Julie was thrilled. Okay, it wasn't Paris, but she would have to change airplanes in Paris, and besides, she was going to be staying with *a real French family*.

Julie burst into The Lounge with more energy than I thought it was possible for such a tiny body to exude. 'Margie!' she panted. 'I have news!' She slowly placed her hands on the table and took a deep breath. 'They have a son.'

Julie explained that she had written to the family, thanking them for their offer and telling them that she was very interested in staying with them, practicing her language skills and immersing herself in the French culture.

'Jules!' I laughed. 'How much immersing are you planning to do in two days?'

Julie ignored me. 'Well, Madame Trignant wrote back and told me a little bit about the family.' She pulled out a letter that was written in English and scanned it. 'Um … it's her and her husband … yada yada yada … live in a converted farmhouse … whatever … here it is! We have a twenty-nine-year-old son, Laurant, who lives with us. He works for Concorde, and he is very excited to meet you and show you around our beautiful town.'

Julie put down the letter and stared at me triumphantly. 'Margie, you have to help me decide, what am I going to wear?'

Chapter 14
Alliances formed and broken in the classroom

Reporting what someone has told you

Il m'a dit que ...	He told me that ...
Il m'a proposé que ...	He proposed to me that ...
Il m'a répondu que ...	He responded to me that ...

Julie's enthusiasm for all things French was peaking. She wanted to be fully linguistically prepared for when she met Laurant, so on the first day of the next semester, Julie turned up having thoroughly revised the last two semesters' work *plus* the work we would be doing in this one. Unfortunately, the planning for her trip coincided with a downward turn in our classes.

To be fair to Claire, she was given a shocking class. Bag Lady was the only person to continue into the next semester with Julie and me and she instantly took a dislike to Claire, who looked as though she stood for everything that Bag Lady detested.

Claire was small, cute and pretty. She had a soft voice and a laugh like a little bell. When she introduced herself, she said, *'J'adore la mode!'* (I love fashion) and you could see Bag Lady squirm in her chair. She then proceeded to show a video on fashion in France and then ask the class questions about it.

We knew from previous lessons that Bag Lady had a real problem with the fashion industry. Quite correctly, she felt that a lot of the garments sold in Australia were produced by women working as indentured slaves in sweatshops. But rather than espousing that people should buy non-sweatshop garments, she decided that fashion in its entirety was evil.

Bag Lady was devastated that Aleksandra was no longer our teacher, and her replacement being a fashion-loving beauty was the final straw. Although nothing out of the ordinary for us, I think that it had taken a lot for Bag Lady to open up and form a friendship with me, Julie and Aleksandra. In the new circumstances, Bag Lady quickly slipped back into her negative, sad personality, and after the second class of the new semester, we never saw her again.

Julie and I were surprised at how much we actually missed Bag Lady, especially as we soon discovered we were now in a mean class with a hopeless teacher. We could tell straightaway that Claire wasn't a very experienced teacher. Her idea of teaching was to get us to read out grammar lessons from the book and then complete the exercises, something we could have done at home and saved the money on classes. When she did need to explain something further, it took her a long time and she wasn't very effective. But she was harmless—which is more than could be said for some of our previous teachers.

Claire's greatest enemy was her voice. It was so small that we all had to strain to understand what she was saying. It also meant that when she was trying to explain a tricky point to a student, she would be talked over and deprived of the opportunity to explain what she meant. She had no control over the class, and if ever there was a class that needed controlling, it was this one.

Once we had realised that at the beginning of every semester there would be at least a couple of new freaks who may or may not last the term, Julie and I began labelling them according to their particular quirks. It started with Bag Lady, and eventually led to the key players in the class.

In appearance, Fräulein was very plain and lacked anything vaguely resembling warmth or personality. She was a buxom woman, although more solid than fat, with a ruddy complexion and lank, blonde hair, without style, that hung halfway down her back. To start, Julie and I called her von Trapp, because of her northern European appearance and harshness, but eventually that was shortened it to Fräulein.

Fräulein seemed to feel inadequate and compensated by intimidating others. She would challenge Claire at every opportunity and often demand that she speak in English. She would scoff at the text the class was reading, which would be about French culture and generally send the message that she was a tough, assertive, no bullshit woman.

Like most bullies, Fräulein set her sights on the weakest targets. There were two older gentlemen in this particular class. Perhaps due to their age, or perhaps due to the fact that it may have been a lifetime since they were last in a classroom, the men were a bit slower than the rest of the class. It took them a little longer to grasp a point and they often had to read over text several times before they understood it.

No matter what their background or personality, students would automatically become brothers in arms. Even if you felt irritated by someone, or not even like them, there are unspoken rules of support. If someone needs a few minutes, extra help, or if they do not understand a concept, you sit back and allow the teacher to help them, because frankly, you would want the same empathy if you were in that situation. Plus, it provides a few minutes of veg-out time.

Fräulein had no such empathy. She would frequently roll her eyes and fidget loudly until the old men became so rattled they abandoned their quest for understanding. In one particular class, one of the older men was struggling. What he was having trouble with was pretty basic, it was a simple verb conjugation, but he just needed a minute to get his head around when to employ it. He was concentrating really hard. When her fidgeting and tongue-clicking proved ineffective, Fräulein threw down her pen and exclaimed, 'Can't we just move on and stop wasting time?'

The old man was humiliated and I was fuming. It was one of those cases where you wish you could go back in time and deliver a retort you have since thought of. In this case, 'No, and considering we spent the first ten minutes of the lesson explaining *passé conditionnel* to you, I think you can let this man have a couple of minutes.' I didn't say that, but the feeling of anger hung in the air.

Claire was another soft target for Fräulein. Claire was physically tiny, with a soft voice and a friendly demeanour. And she had no control over the class. This wasn't really a problem; after all, we were all adults who rarely got out of hand. The only time it became an issue was when

Fräulein would boom demands for explanations from Claire and you could almost see Claire physically cower.

Intermediate 5 concentrated on reportage, the explaining of an event or conversation that had happened in the past. It doesn't sound difficult, but it is. Reportage is the same as it is in English, but that doesn't make it easier, because it requires the use of several different verb conjugations in the one sentence.

The only easy part is that the beginning is almost always the same: 'He said that ...' 'He demanded that ...' et cetera. The only way to learn reportage is practice. *Devoirs maison*, or homework, for Intermediate 5, generally consisted of a series of statements that we had to turn into reportage.

During one class, we were correcting the homework and we went around the class each reading out one answer. An example might be, 'He washes his car', and Julie would read it out as 'He said that he has been washing his car'. Then it was my turn. 'He did no study', I read it out as 'He said that he had not studied'. Even the old men did well. There was a feeling of accomplishment in the class. Until it came to Fräulein.

Her statement was, 'He will win the election'. The answer, of course, should have been 'He said that he will win the election'. The response Fräulein gave was, 'He will win the election'.

'No', Claire corrected, in French, 'you must say, "he said that he will win the election".'

'No, you don't have to say that', Fräulein replied firmly. Julie and I relaxed back in our chairs. This was going to take a few minutes and for a little while the pressure would be off us.

'Yes, you do', explained Claire. 'You are reporting what this person says, so you must always start with, he said that ...'

But Fräulein stuck to her guns. By her reasoning, the fact that this person was going to win the election was clear and that was all that mattered. She totally missed the point that we were practicing reportage. Claire became more and more flustered as she tried to explain and Fräulein became more angry to the point where she was on her feet shouting.

Eventually, Claire switched to English in a last attempt to get Fräulein to understand. But this was no longer about French or reportage, this was about winning and Fräulein was not about to admit defeat. Eventually, Fräulein threw up her hands and exclaimed, 'Well, I think you are wrong, you think I am wrong, we're never going to agree, so let's just forget it'.

To our shock, Claire flew into a rage. 'It's not a case of agreeing', she yelled. 'This is the way it is done and if you don't understand it, then you have a big problem!' The class was gobsmacked by this unexpected outburst and Claire appeared to be physically defeated. With shaking hands she turned on a video and for the rest of the lesson the class watched a documentary about Paris landmarks.

Even without aggressive classmates, learning another language can be a frightening experience. You may be a mature woman, at the pinnacle of your career, successfully managing work and family, but once you step into the classroom you are ten years old again.

In most cases you only understand a fraction of what is going on and you are surrounded by people who are better than you. Teachers who are a good deal younger than you will ask you questions you don't even understand, let alone know how to respond to. You wonder if you're good enough and whether you're ever going to understand. Worse still, you're on your own.

As a result of all this terror people form alliances with other students very quickly and in some cases alliances are formed that people later regret. Miranda was one of the ones who made an alliance in haste and repented at leisure.

By the time Julie and I turned up to the first lesson of Intermediate 5 (twenty minutes late as usual), Miranda had formed an alliance with Fräulein. In fairness, it was an easy decision to make. The only other people Miranda had to choose from were the two older men, and they were already in the throes of forming an alliance themselves.

Miranda's name wasn't actually Miranda. We just called her that because she reminded us of Miranda from *Sex and the City*: late thirties, conservative dress and haircut, probably in upper–middle management.

Our guess was that she was learning French because she thought it was a little bit exotic and the rest of her life was not.

Miranda's French was quite advanced, she had an excellent speaking voice. She didn't always understand the ins and outs of reportage, but she didn't seem too stressed about it. I'm sure Fräulein appealed to her because she, too, thought of herself as an assertive power woman. Fräulein and Miranda sat next to each other in every class. Together, they contributed to each other's arguments and questions and in the true spirit of an alliance, backed each other up when they felt the other person's question was being misunderstood.

The Fräulein–Miranda alliance began to come unstuck around the time Fräulein savaged the old man and was completely dissolved when Fräulein upset Claire. I don't think Miranda had a moral objection to the way Fräulein treated everyone, I think mainly she was embarrassed by it. Occasionally, when Fräulein was being obnoxious Miranda would look over to Julie and me and giggle nervously. Then, more and more, she began talking to us after the class. She clearly wanted to distance herself from Fräulein, but it was too late.

Julie and I formed an alliance unto ourselves and if Miranda had been smart she would have realised that and not even attempted infiltration. There was just something about Miranda we didn't like and we realised what it was at the end of the last class when we were discussing re-enrolling for the following semester. 'I'm going to book over the Internet so I can see who else is going to be in the class', she announced. She had more in common with Fräulein than we realised, and she was already looking to make a new alliance.

Chapter 15
Trouble at gURLpool and Julie falls in love

Opposition

Malgré + nom
Il travaille malgré son grand âge.
He works despite his advanced age.

En dépit de
Elle se bronze en dépit de tout conseil.
She sunbakes despite all advice.

Et pourtant
Je suis malade et pourtant je travaille.
I am sick and nevertheless I am working.

Just as the tension and stress in French class was growing, things were becoming a little more relaxed at work—at least temporarily. When Sarah took a month off work to go on vacation, Maeve and I breathed a sigh of relief. Sarah had been much calmer since gURLpool had moved to a new office but, while she was away, Maeve and I would be able to get on with our work without her interference and poorly timed demands.

Unable to survive financially as an independently operating magazine, gURLpool had been sold to a Gift Rapt, a corporate gifting company that was expanding its operations to include online services. It wasn't such a bad thing. The new owners offered us financial backing and also security that gURLpool had never had before. More importantly, they didn't want to change the format or content of gURLpool at all.

Editorially it would stay the same; the only difference was the shopping pages now took the readers to their site alone. The role of gURLpool was simply to drive traffic to their site and they understood it was in their best interests to keep gURLpool as it was to maintain its popularity.

However, the problem was that Gift Rapt was essentially a shop and not a magazine and the owners and management had no understanding of the particular needs and requirements of a magazine. This became apparent on the day we arrived at the new premises only to discover that one phone had been allocated to three journalists and an editor. Things progressively became worse when we were asked to do things, like helping out in the warehouse in busy times and were ostracised when we refused because we were on a deadline.

In her year at gURLpool, Maeve's attitude to work had not improved. She still took criticism as a personal attack and reacted like someone under fire, digging her heels in, challenging Sarah's authority and complaining loudly and aggressively. The move to Gift Rapt had simply given her a new reason to feel disgruntled. Going to Gift Rapt did bring us closer together, though. Maeve was constantly stressed about her work and the level of respect she received, but in all other areas she was a hoot.

The gURLpool editorial team was treated with suspicion and distrust when we first arrived. The Gift Rapt employees were a tight group of young uni graduates who were no doubt intimidated by the pashminas and designer handbags they saw when we first walked in. The situation was made worse by the fact that they didn't really understand why we were there. In the end it was Maeve who was largely responsible for breaking down the barriers. Her bawdy jokes and ability to take the piss out of herself—and us—meant that the people at Gift Rapt soon warmed to us. On Friday evenings Sarah would leave for Sabbath dinner and I would leave to go home and study, but Maeve would join the staff of Gift Rapt at the pub and get horribly drunk and hilarious.

The day before she left on vacation, Sarah sent an email to Maeve and me. It was very encouraging, saying that she had complete confidence we would put out a fantastic issue (although this upset Maeve, 'What does she think we are, juniors? Has she forgotten that I used to edit the *Green Guide*?') and she was not going to appoint an acting editor. 'I want you to edit each other's work and you can both help to write the editor's letter', she wrote.

For the next few weeks Maeve was happy, and together we had a lot of fun. Instead of seeing her job as a constant reminder that she wasn't appreciated, she was able to laugh and hold her head up high—and be in charge of her own writing and editorial decisions.

The week before Christmas, an email was sent to all Gift Rapt staff, informing us that we would be required to work in the warehouse for an hour every day. A copy of the roster was attached. For most people it was a minor inconvenience and interruption to their work, but for Maeve and I it would mean the difference between getting the issue out on time or not.

Again, Maeve took this as a personal affront. 'I'm a journalist, for God's sake!' she cried. 'Not a fucking factory worker. They have got no idea. *No idea!*'

Actually, I agreed with her more than a little. It was humiliating to be stuck in a stinking hot warehouse with a group of twenty-year-old uni graduates who believed all the hype that through this dotcom they were standing on the cutting edge of a societal revolution. They didn't care that they were packing boxes, they just wanted to be a part of it.

Maeve and I discussed it and sent an email to management saying that we were on a deadline and were understaffed as it was. If we had to work in the warehouse we wouldn't be able to get the issue out on time and fulfil our obligations to the advertisers. Thankfully, we were excused.

But that hiccup set Maeve off on a mission to show everyone—me, Sarah, everyone at Gift Rapt, gURLpool readers—that she was so much greater than we all thought. It started when she was editing my articles. Rather than just correcting the typos and rearranging the odd sentence, Maeve sent back her corrections with detailed explanations as to which rule of grammar or spelling I had ignored, and a note urging me to take more care in future. As usual I just ignored it. I didn't care what Maeve thought. I knew she had issues and figured I'd just sit it out.

As we were editing articles and choosing pictures for the new issue, Ben was gradually putting the new website together. A couple of days before the upload I opened the test site to have a quick look at how it was going. I flicked through the different channels, all in various states of completion, and then I clicked on the editor's letter. I expected to see a big, empty space, because we hadn't written it yet. Instead, I saw an editor's letter. One I hadn't seen before. One that was signed by Maeve, acting editor.

Maeve was sitting right next to me in earshot, so I emailed Ben asking him what was the deal with the editor's letter. He replied that Maeve had sent it to him the other day. He had apparently asked if I had seen it and Maeve had replied that I didn't need to, and she was actually doing me a favour by not including me on it because I was so busy.

I was furious, but at a complete loss as to what to do. I went outside and smoked a cigarette in record time while I considered my options. I soon realised I didn't have many. There was no-one to whom I could complain, or who might tell Maeve to take off her editor's letter and replace it with a joint one. It never occurred to me that I should be the one to do it.

I was angry with Maeve because she was depriving me of the little recognition I got for all my hard work, all the extra work I put in and also because she had pulled a swiftie on me. Up until now, Maeve and I had been allies at work. We were the ones with at least one foot in reality and we had laughed together on numerous occasions. She was one of the reasons I loved coming to work—she was professional and a great writer, and as the only other full-time journalist, we were in the same boat. I knew she had insecurities about work, which had caused her to lash out at people in the past, but I never thought I would be on the receiving end of them.

I wanted to go back upstairs and tell Maeve that I did not appreciate her going behind my back and that we would have to replace the editor's letter with one which we would do together, but I was too scared and too unwilling to deal with the consequences. I decided to ignore it and let Sarah deal with it.

When Sarah came back from holidays, she went through the site and was, surprisingly, not too critical. She did notice the editor's letter, though. The next day Maeve and I arrived at work to 'Please explain' emails. I don't know what Maeve's response was, but I imagine it was the same she gave Ben. I wrote to Sarah telling her exactly what I saw happen—Maeve hijacked the editor's letter. A few minutes later, Sarah asked to see Maeve outside. When they came back, Maeve looked furious.

Everyone worked in silence until Sarah went out to lunch. Then Maeve confronted me. 'Did you tell Sarah that I wouldn't let you contribute to the editor's letter?' she demanded angrily.

'Well, I didn't use those words!' I retorted. 'I just said you wrote it and uploaded it without consulting me ...'

'Okay', she said with controlled anger. 'It's true that I wanted to look like I edited the site, but I am the more qualified editor. If it wasn't for me all those mistakes you made would be on the site, and what thanks do I get? This!' The way Maeve was talking, I should have been grateful to her for covering for my weaknesses and should have been ashamed for dobbing her in to Sarah.

I was torn between being cross at her for the way she was speaking to me and feeling sorry for her. Maeve had such great wit and personality and I was genuinely fond of her. So I sat there and took it.

Not long afterwards, Gift Rapt went the way of many dotcoms. The investors got scared at the amount of money they were losing and ordered Gift Rapt to cut staff. More than half the staff were retrenched and gURLpool was told it had to lose one journalist. Sarah chose Maeve to leave.

★★★★

While I got to keep my job, I was exhausted. It seemed as though every day at gURLpool was a new drama or a new clash of personalities. And French lessons were providing no relief. In fact, French was adding to the conflict that seemed to be becoming a prominent part of my life. Since their argument in the first class, Claire and Fräulein had been locked in battle. Claire would explain some rule of grammar and Fräulein would challenge relentlessly, trying to find any weak point in Claire's teaching method. It never happened, because Claire would always retaliate with a complicated explanation, trying to prove that Fräulein just didn't understand. Neither would concede on any point, no matter how trivial. Julie and I were spending almost all of the class in silence, letting the drama happen around us. And we were learning practically nothing.

While I blamed Maeve and Sarah and most of Gift Rapt, as well as the students in my class, in reality I was not proud of the way I was handling myself. Sure I was surviving retrenchment and persisting with French, but I was so passive. Maeve was right, I rarely stood up for myself and the truth was I wasn't sure I knew how.

Julie, by contrast, was handling herself extremely well. For someone who at first glance appeared to be quiet and refined, she was suddenly displaying extreme assertiveness. Julie had written a letter to Laurant under the pretext of introducing herself, and in it had included a photo of herself. 'So he knows what I look like when he picks me up from the airport', she pouted defensively. I'm not sure how asking him if he had a girlfriend was going to help in the identification process, but his response sent Julie into a frenzy of French lust.

'I do not have a girlfriend. I did have a girlfriend but we broke up last year. She did not want a boyfriend, I think. Someday I would like to be married to a beautiful woman and have a family.'

The business trip was still several months away, but Julie and Laurant were writing letters to each other every week. And every weekend, Julie would turn up to the pub with her French homework plus the latest letter from Laurant, and we would do our homework and dissect the hidden meanings in what he wrote—the latter occupying the vast majority of our time and our efforts.

'… On the weekend I went to the cinema with my friends. I also went shopping and bought some CDs and went to the gymnasium …'

Laurant said he liked going to the gym, which we took to mean that he had a hot body. He had dark, curly hair, which we interpreted to mean he was a spunk. And, he liked going to the movies and listening to music, which we took to mean he had the same interests as Julie. 'Plus,' I pointed out, 'he speaks perfect English and works for Concorde, so he must be very smart'.

After several weeks, it became clear that Julie was falling in love. She carried herself with a calmness and serenity I had never seen in her before and sometimes she would laugh to herself and then explain, 'Oh, I was just thinking of something funny that Laurant wrote'.

I really did admire the way that Julie had turned what was originally a short business trip to London into a situation where she was standing on the brink of having her romantic fantasies realised. I, on the other hand, felt as though I was for the most part standing back from my life and letting everything happen around me. I resolved to be more assertive at work, and going into the next semester of French, I vowed that, no matter who the teacher or classmates were, I would actively turn it around to be an enjoyable and fruitful experience.

Chapter 16
The girls meet Yann, the teacher who saves them

Fear, worry, joy and contentment

Craindre	to fear
S'effrayer	to become frightened
L'angoisse	anguish
Une épreuve	an ordeal
La joie	joy
Joyeux	joyous, joyful
Le bonheur	happiness
Se plaire	to like, enjoy
Un éclat de rire	a burst of laughter

Towards the end of Intermediate 5, Julie and I enrolled for the next semester. We hadn't been terribly impressed with Claire. It was nothing personal, she was sweet, but we just wanted Aleksandra back. Julie and I wanted a return to the days when we could laugh and joke with the teacher, talk about movies and sleazy men and be in more control of what we were learning.

Sitting behind the front desk was Jean-Philippe, the director of the Alliance Française. Students and teachers came and went at the Alliance, but the one constant was Jean-Philippe. He had been the director for years and was a big part of life at the Alliance. He hosted all the events, and could be seen at any time sitting in his office or working behind the desk.

Neither Julie nor I had ever said much to Jean-Philippe, mainly because he was quite scary. Physically, he was very tall and intimidating and when he spoke his voice boomed through the building. No matter what the situation, he always had an intense expression on his face, and whenever a teacher spoke of him, it was always with a great deal of reverence.

Our faces fell when Jean-Philippe told us matter-of-factly that Aleksandra wasn't taking any intermediate classes. Our new teacher was named Yann. Despondent, we walked away from the reception desk. As we walked to the exit we passed the whiteboard that listed the classes in progress, what rooms they were in and who the teachers were. Yann, whoever he was, was currently taking a class in *Salle* 3. We had to get a look at him.

Unfortunately, looking through the glass panels of the door in Room 3 would require us to position ourselves behind the reception desk and press our faces against the door; not something that would go unnoticed by either Jean-Philippe or Yann. Undeterred, Julie and I decided to peak into the windows that led onto the garden.

Darkness was our friend. The Alliance has an unspoken rule about their gardens, which is the same as the laws governing parks in Paris: the highly manicured grass is for admiring, not for setting foot on. As it was late in the evening, Julie and I figured we could sneak right up to the window undetected.

What we hadn't counted on was the fact that the building is set high above the gardens and the windows high up the walls. The only way we were going to see what this Yann looked like was if we jumped. So we did. Unfortunately, at the height of each leap we could only catch a glimpse of the teacher.

'*Il porte des lunettes!*' I exclaimed as I landed.

'*Il a une moustache!*' Julie whispered as she landed.

The humour of what we were doing, the descriptions of Yann, and imagining what the students would think if they caught glimpses of two heads leaping up to the window left us in uncontrollable fits of laughter. We aborted our mission when the sensor lights in the garden were activated and we were exposed.

When we got to the car we tried to fit together an image of Yann, based on the snippets we had seen. We felt like police officers compiling a photo identikit. He was in his mid forties, wore glasses and wore a moustache or possibly a beard and looked serious, but not intimidating.

Two weeks later, on the first night of class, we learnt that we had looked in the wrong classroom or the whiteboard had been fibbing, but whoever that man we had spied on was, he certainly hadn't been Yann. At the front of the classroom stood a different man, who introduced himself as Yann. Julie and I instantly fell in love. Not in a passionate, 'let me rip your clothes off and tamper with you' way, but more in the way of 'let me take you home for a feed and a cuddle'. 'We love Yann!' Julie and I would croon in chorus with a dreamy look on our faces whenever we'd think about Yann, or whenever he would do something cute. Which was often.

Yann was adorable. He was shortish and plumpish, and you wouldn't look twice at him in the street. Yet, what he lacked in height he made up for in personality. Julie and I loved him from the first class. Yann began by introducing himself and he was so sweet and humble. He asked us if we would mind him calling us *tu* instead of *vous*, which had never happened before.

Then he told us that he planned to build up our confidence. 'The biggest obstacle for learning another language is *confiance*', he explained. 'When my wife was learning French she used to come home frustrated and angry because she didn't understand something. That's bad because if you don't love a language you will never be able to learn a language. I want you to love French!'

'Yay', Julie and I silently cheered. We wanted to love French too! Yann explained that he wanted the classes to be fun and that he wanted to nurture an environment where no-one was intimidated and everyone could express themselves. 'If there is a person who doesn't understand something, we all stop and help them', he explained. 'No-one will be left behind and it is also good because when you explain something to another person, you understand it more.'

It was exactly what we needed to hear and Julie and I struggled to hold back tears of joy, while silently swearing undying devotion to Yann. He could not have come into our lives at a better time. Our *confiance* had taken a battering in the last semester. We had yet to understand what we were supposed to have learnt, largely as a result of Claire's lack of teaching ability, and we had seen what Fräulein and Miranda did to people who dared to hold up the class. Yann was our saviour.

One by one we introduced ourselves the usual way: name, occupation, why we are learning French—and Yann looked on as though what we were saying was the most interesting thing he had heard all day.

J'étudie le français parce que j'aime la musique française', explained Julie. '*Vanessa Paradis …*' Suddenly Yann let out a high-pitched screeching noise and we all jumped. He was singing a Vanessa Paradis song—like Vanessa Paradis.

That was one of the most endearing things about Yann. He was quite prepared to make a fool of himself to help us relax. Watching Yann teach was like watching live theatre. He was flamboyant and expressive but not in an intimidating way like Xavier.

In one class he told us how he had come to live in Australia. He met an Australian girl in France and they decided to marry. She brought him home to Sydney and he explained to us what happened, with the use of actions and sound effects.

'There I was, my first day in Australia, at a barbecue.' (Insert turning sausage action and sound effects of sizzling.) 'They say, "would you like a beer?"' (Insert action of opening a can, along with the ke-chew sound of opening the said can.) 'There's the sun, the sky, the Opera House in the backyard …"' (Insert dreamy expression.) 'And the most beautiful woman in the world saying, "Would you like to live in Australia?"' He shook his head solemnly. Clearly there was no other option but to move to Australia.

Not only did Julie and I love Yann but Yann loved us, too. We were his favourites. He laughed his head off at the stories we would make up for our homework and he was always interested in what we had to say. Even Fräulein and Miranda loved Yann and they always behaved themselves for fear of him not loving them back.

Yann really made the class feel he was giving his all. He even made an apology on nights he was 'a little flat'. One night in particular he was a little flat because he had accidentally made a young girl cry.

Every year the Alliance hosts a poetry reading for primary and high school students. The students from participating schools are asked to memorise a short poem, which they have been given. The Alliance then sends teachers out to the schools to sit all day and listen to recitals.

The procedure is that a student walks into the room and begins by introducing themselves, 'Bonjour, je m'appelle …', or something similar. The teacher ticks off their name and the student begins to read. This day, Yann had been listening to young girls all day and he was a bit tired and bored. Then a girl walked in and said, 'Bonjour, Je m'appelle'. Then she started reading the poem.

'Wait!' Yann interrupted. 'You must tell me your name?'

'Je m'appelle', replied the girl.

'No, your name?' Yann stressed.

'Je m'appelle', the girl insisted.

Yann was beginning to lose his cool. Apparently this went on for some time until the girl was sniffling, holding back tears. Yann went to speak to her teacher and learnt the student's name was actually Jemma Pell.

Chapter 17
An intimate lesson with Yann

Getting around

Je voudrais aller à …	I would like to go to …
Pour aller à …	How do I get to …
C'est loin?	Is it far?
Quelle est l'heure d'ouverture?	What time does it open?
Je voudrais un billet …	I would like a ticket …

Everyone was going to Paris for the summer—at least that was how it seemed to me. My sister, Liz, had been living in Quebec for a couple of years, where she was studying French-to-English translation. She had just started her first job as a translator at the Australian Embassy in Paris. It was summer in Paris and the Australian Bar Association was holding its annual convention in the capital. My stepfather Barry, a judge, was planning to attend the convention with my mother, who was taking the opportunity to visit Liz.

One day I was sitting on my mother's bed complaining to her about work and the problems I was experiencing with Gift Rapt. After two years, I wanted something else. gURLpool was completely different from the way it was when I started. It looked and read the same, and the readership was still as healthy as ever, but we were operating on a skeleton staff, in a company that was essentially a shop. For all her irritating ways, I learnt a lot from Sarah and the other journalists. We fed off each other, shared story ideas, and knew what we were all going through in the course of our jobs. But it had become enough just to get an issue out on time. Maeve was gone and Sarah was part-time.

Sarah had been approached by a very prestigious UK film magazine to write a series of star profiles. She wanted to dedicate as much time and effort to it as possible, believing that after she submitted the commissioned articles, the magazine would want to hire her on a regular basis. Plus, if she couldn't be a star herself, the next best thing for Sarah would be spending her days hanging out with them. Yet, Sarah wasn't ready to give up the prestige of heading up gURLpool, so she decided to simply cut her hours down.

What this meant for me was a dramatically increased workload. The pay-off was that I was given the title of Editor, while Sarah became Editor At Large. Although I had never really harboured an ambition to be editor, once in the job I found it exciting. There was a lot of responsibility and pressure—the success or failure of an edition depended on the decisions I made, and I loved the control and felt proud of every issue that went live. But it was around-the-clock work and I hadn't had a break since starting work at gURLpool. Before long I was feeling tired and fed up. Suddenly, Mum's face lit up. 'Come to Paris with me and Barry', she said. 'You'll get to see Liz! We'll all be together! It will be great!'

I was doubtful. Weren't overseas trips something you spent months planning? Not to mention saving up for? Julie had been planning and saving for her two-day trip to France for months. The bar convention was less than a month away but Mum wasn't having any of it. 'We'll book your ticket on the Internet', she said, turning on her computer. And that, it seemed, was that.

Julie was thrilled that I was going to Paris. 'You have to tell me what all the French girls are wearing', she instructed. 'I need to know what I should wear during the day *and* at night. Laurant is taking me to a bar *and* a restaurant, so I need to know for *both* of those places.'

Money was going to be a problem though, so I decided to reduce the costs of the holiday the best way journalists know how. I would write a couple of stories, and write the trip off as a tax deduction. I had been thinking for some months that what I would ideally like to do would be to work part-time at gURLpool and write freelance for other publications for the rest of the time. If I went to France I could gather story ideas for my freelance work and practice my French. I would still be a journalist but I would be working in France.

Part Two: Intermediate

Immediately, I thought of two article ideas I could sell to some magazine, or at least write for gURLpool—one on French food and one on French fashion. But I also decided to go out on a limb and email PR agencies that represented French actors and musicians. I already had a few articles on French actors published, so I felt fairly confident I could do some more. Plus, I had tangible examples of my work to show the other agencies.

I fully expected not to hear back from many. It was summer in France, so a lot of celebrities were away on holiday. The ones who weren't could just have easily been away working on a film, or just too busy. Then there was the fact that I was working for an Australian magazine and may not have been given the same priority as the French publications.

To my astonishment, one of the stories I most wanted was the one that came up—the actor and singer, Patrick Bruel. He had a new album out and was about to embark on a concert tour of Europe. His record company, BMG, was looking for all the publicity they could get.

On top of that, two magazines commissioned me almost immediately to write articles based on my trip—one Australian and the other an Irish publication. I figured that I could write a few articles for gURLpool while I was away, but gURLpool really needed someone who was going to be in Australia to assist with putting the magazine together.

Sarah was only part-time and, aside from the articles we both wrote, the rest of the content was supplied by freelancers and we needed someone to commission them. The Gift Rapt programmers and designers were doing a fabulous job, but they didn't know a thing about managing the editorial side of the magazine or how to put together the look and feel of a magazine.

Often, I would ask for something very basic to be added or changed in the magazine—for example, a typo corrected or a photo credit put in—and they would take their time, or mumble something about me being 'anal'. They simply didn't understand that when you worked on a professional publication these things are considered crucial. In their eyes, I was a perfectionist and someone prone to hissy fits.

I met with David, the director of gURLpool, to discuss how this was going to work. He was thrilled that I was going to Paris. We had become quite close and he knew how happy I was to finally be going. Plus, I was going to file several stories from Paris, which would really add kudos to the magazine—after all, in the world of women's magazines, Paris rules.

'I don't know how you feel about this,' David ventured cautiously, 'and of course you can say no. You are the editor and I do respect that …' He sounded like he was worried I was going to overreact. Since becoming editor, I had noticed that staff at Gift Rapt had begun to tiptoe around me and couch suggestions in the gentlest of terms. Sarah, I gathered, had been quite assertive and vocal with her ideas.

'Why don't we ask Julie if she would like to work for gURLpool?' he continued. 'She could write a fashion feature every month. Our readers would love it. What do you think?'

'I think that's an excellent idea!' I practically shouted. I didn't know why I hadn't thought of it before. It was the perfect solution. Hiring Julie as a journalist wasn't just a case of jobs for friends. Because of her aspirations to become a fashion journalist, Julie had written a couple of articles for gURLpool for free. It was a win–win situation, Julie could build up her folio of published work and I could stay within my budget. Julie had already completed a part-time course in feature writing and was showing a real flair for writing. I think David and the owners of gURLpool were also pleased when Julie joined the team because they thought having a friend to work with might help them retain me.

I called Julie straightaway on her mobile. 'I can't talk for long, lovie,' she said, 'I'm in the car'.

'Okay', I said. 'I want to ask you a quick question. And you can say no if you want to—don't feel pressured at all.'

'Okay', she responded suspiciously.

'We want to hire a part-time fashion writer for gURLpool and I thought it would be great if you did it.' No response.

'I mean, it doesn't pay much,' I continued, 'and take your time to think about it but you'll have the title of fashion editor, plus you'll be able to attend all the shows at fashion week …'

Part Two: Intermediate

'Oh Margie', Julie cried. 'I don't even have to think about it. Yes, yes, yes!'

With that, Julie let out a giant sob and hung up.

★★★★

The best class of our entire Alliance experience was thanks to Yann, and the other class members who failed to show up. It was just me and Julie in the class and when it became clear that no-one else was coming, Yann slammed the textbook shut and announced that we weren't going to work from the book. With a mischevious grin he told us that we were going to play a little game instead.

He disappeared for a few minutes, we assumed to get the props required for this game and Julie and I giggled and spoke nervously. It was a mixture of 'Oh my God, it's going to be something really hard!' and 'Oh my God, we're playing a game with Yann!'

Yann returned a few minutes later with a map of Paris.

'This is a game especially for the girls who are going to Paris!' he announced. Julie and I giggled like teenagers because he was talking about us. 'After this game you will have so much confidence, it will be fantastic.'

In this game, Julie and I would be on vacation in Paris. We would have to describe where we were going and how we got there and what we were doing. Along the way, he explained, we would run into various people and he would play their role.

Julie and I were nervous. First we had to decide where we were going to stay. We decided on the area of l'Opéra because it was close to two large shopping centres. The game started with us checking in. Yann was the concierge, and the persona he adopted was polite and formal. It was a five-star hotel after all.

Yann's greeting was very rapid. The only thing we understood was that it had ended in a question, because Yann had his eyebrows raised as though he expected a response. Julie and I looked at him blankly and said nothing.

'Okay', said Yann, in English. 'I will talk just like the French and you must act just like you were in Paris. What would you say if you didn't understand what someone said?'

'*Répétez-vous, s'il vous plaît?*' offered Julie.

'*Doucement, s'il vous plaît?*' I added.

'*Exactement!*' said Yann. 'Now go!' he said and repeated what he had previously said.

'*Répétez-vous doucement, s'il vous plaît?*' asked Julie. Damn, I thought, major brownie points for Julie for combining the two statements.

Dutifully, Yann repeated the statement, slowly. This time we were able to pick out a few words and deduced that the concierge was asking whether we would like breakfast in our room, what we would like and whether we would like it added to the bill. Easy! We moved on.

Naturally, the first stop Julie and I made was to the Champs Élysées for a spot of shopping. We walked there because it wasn't far, judging by the map, and walked into Louis Vuitton to buy a handbag. Yann suddenly transformed into a camp sales assistant. We told him we wanted a bag and described it. '*Petit, mais pas trop petit*', began Julie. '*Comme le sac que Kate Moss a porté aux Oscars*', I added.

Yann took this request with all the seriousness of a gay sales assistant working at Louis Vuitton. He was mortified to inform us that they were currently out of stock. We stressed the importance of this particular handbag and he told us that he would order one from another store and have it by this afternoon. This was fun!

After a tough morning shopping, Julie and I decided we needed to '*prendre un pot*'. We caught the Metro to St Germain des Près and walked into a restaurant. Yann momentarily turned his back on us. When he spun around he had his jumper tied around his waist like an apron and his scarf draped across his bent arm like a tea towel. He had become the waiter from hell.

He ranted and raved about the specials and described the menu as though our very existence was a waste of his time. But our confidence was peaking and we knew exactly what we wanted so we were able to keep him in place.

Next we went to Père Lachaise cemetery. It wasn't easy to get to and required three different Metro lines. By the time we had checked out the grave sites of Jean-Paul Sartre, Jim Morrison and Chopin, we realised we were not going to have time to get to Louis Vuitton to get our handbags. We decided to phone and ask them to deliver the bags to our hotel.

Yann turned his back to us and answered the phone in the manner of the flamboyant gay guy. I tried to explain what I wanted, but the sales assistant kept talking to other shoppers and mumbling under his breath something about dumb Americans. Despite my *Je peux t'entendre!* (I can hear you!), he wouldn't let me speak.

Eventually I blurted out, *'Il faut que vous mettiez nos sacs à l'hotel!'* (It is absolutely necessary for you to send our bags to the hotel.) *Il faut que …* is a top expression to know. Not only is it powerfully insistent, it requires use of the dreaded subjunctive.

Yann spun around in a state of heightened arousal. 'Voila!' he cried. 'You have got it! I knew as soon as you said *'Il faut que'* that you will be perfectly fine in Paris!'

It took hours to get to sleep that night. We were so wound up and excited. For the first time, we felt like we were actually prepared to go into the advanced courses.

★★★★

It seemed to me that work at gURLpool became infinitely more fun with Julie on board, especially during fashion week. Julie took to her new role with gusto. Financially, it was necessary for her to continue working at the bank, but she spent her lunchtimes visiting designers, attending the openings of new stores and picking up and dropping off stock to photograph. When they appeared on the site, her articles were bright and sassy.

Julie embraced fashion week with the same enthusiasm and determination as the French film festival. Together we mapped out the shows we would attend. Normally, I would go to the first one after work and then go home, but Julie would often stay for two or three shows.

The excitement and glamour of fashion week can be intoxicating—the gorgeous clothes, loud music and celebrity models all create an atmosphere of electricity. Julie simply adored it. But you didn't have to look far beneath the surface of champagne, canapés and gift bags to see an ugly side to fashion week. Cold-faced women bitching about who got a better seat at what show would check out what you wore before asking, 'Who do you work for?' The great thing about doing fashion week with Julie was that we loved the fashion but were able to laugh at the show of it all. Together, Julie and I were not the slightest bit intimidated and we knew we always looked great—but in private we weren't kidding ourselves.

'Thank you, good night', we said seriously to the doorman as he handed us each a gift bag—a bag of products to thank the media for coming to the show. We took our gift bags without even looking at them and walked out into the street.

'Hmm, feels kind of heavy', Julie muttered without opening her mouth as we walked to the car.

'Yes', I mumbled back. 'But I'm a bit worried about the size ...'

Julie stifled a laugh. As soon as we turned the corner and were out of sight of other fashion week invitees, we ripped open our bags and searched through the goodies. We were very excited about the free make-up and other beauty products, but we understood that becoming excited was something one just didn't do at fashion week. At fashion week it's important to sound terribly chic but look as though you couldn't care less.

One night, Julie decided to skip the last show and come home with me. She had looked a little flat all evening.

'Is everything alright?' I asked on the trip home.

'It's Laurant', she sighed.

'Oh man!' I mocked. 'Don't tell me you two are going to split up before you've even met!'

Julie laughed. 'I don't know,' she said, 'he seems so perfect. He's smart and funny and cultured and he's really into me. In every letter he wants to know what I am doing and how I am feeling. He's just ... perfect'.

Part Two: Intermediate
125

'And he's French, don't forget', I added.

'I know, I know.' Julie laughed. Then her face became serious and she turned to me. 'Margie, he doesn't know who Tom Ford is.'

'What are you doing writing to him about Tom Ford?' I asked. I was bewildered as to why Julie would have been discussing the fashion designer for Gucci with Laurant.

'Margie.' Julie sighed. 'We write to each other about everything. I mean pages and pages every week. And I told him that I worship Tom Ford.' She paused. 'He wrote back and asked if that was my boyfriend.'

'Oh dear.' I giggled. Sensing that Julie was not amused I got serious. 'Jules, this is not a problem. So he doesn't know anything about fashion designers—what guy does? It doesn't matter! You don't have to have everything in common. Look at Lincoln and me. He doesn't care the slightest bit about fashion or anything else that I write about for that matter, but that's not a problem. Jules, when it comes to choosing a life partner, having similar interests is such a minor consideration.'

Julie didn't look appeased. 'What else?' I asked warily.

Julie looked up at me with moist eyes. 'Margie, he went on a date.'

I didn't know what to say.

'In his last letter he wrote all the things he did on the weekend and one of them was that he had a date.'

'Who with? What kind of date was it?'

'I don't know!' replied Julie. 'He just said on Sunday night he went on a date. That's it! No explanation, no nothing!'

'Jules, that doesn't mean anything', I reassured her. 'It could have been anything. He could have misused the word date. You know,' I added, 'he may not have even gone on a date. He might have just said that to make himself look desirable in your eyes. You know, I think that's it. That's why he didn't give any details—because there were none!'

'That could be true,' Julie said, looking brighter. 'I know he is a good man. He's got the same values as me—family, career, honesty, and he *is* French!'

★★★★

How to Be French

I think Yann was more excited by my trip than I was. He was certainly into the whole Patrick Bruel thing.

The week following my announcement that I was going to Paris and writing a story about Patrick Bruel, Yann brought a video cassette of French music to class and played *Au Café des Délices*, a song from Bruel's last CD. 'What did you think of it?' he asked the class afterwards. 'What do you think about the video? Yalil yalil, habibi yalil', he sang.

It was the second last week before I was due to go away, and as we were packing up at the end of the class Yann said, 'Okay, next week we will together write a letter to Patrick Bruel'. He said it very rapidly and in French so I wasn't quite sure I had heard correctly. Other people in the class were smiling. I was beginning to panic.

'Think about what you would like to say to him,' Yann continued, 'and Margie will give him the letter'.

'That will be fun', said Miranda. 'Maybe he'll write back.'

This was the second time that Julie or I shared The Look. The first time was when Julie was bombarded by questions in Intermediate 6. Now it was my turn. My face showed a smile but was paralysed with disbelief—only my eyes showed panic.

'Yes,' continued Yann, 'we'll write it together and sign it from the Thursday night class at the Alliance Française de Melbourne.'

Bugger the French, I needed to put a stop to this right away. 'Yann,' I demanded in English, 'are you saying you want me to give Patrick Bruel a letter signed by the Thursday night class at the Alliance Française de Melbourne?' I almost shrieked.

'But of course', said Yann. 'It will be so great ...'

'Yann, I don't want to look like a dickhead!'

Julie couldn't contain her laughter and burst into hysterics. Yann's face turned stony and he said, 'Oh, you don't want to look like a dickhead? What do you think I do every week? I come in here and I look like a dickhead. Yalil yalil, habibi yalil. If I look like a dickhead, you can look like a dickhead.'

Julie kept laughing all the way home. 'God love him!' She shook her head, smiling.

Although Julie and I adored Yann, it wasn't sexual. It was more a strange attachment that students form with the teachers they feel comfortable with, and a tender friendship between like-minded individuals. There was only ever one fleeting moment of sexual tension.

We were discussing art. The conversation was harmless enough and not even particularly funny. Yann was telling us about his love for the classics and walked up to the Monet print on the wall behind us. 'Do you like this?' he asked, directing the question at me.

Contrary to what it may seem like to an outsider, that wasn't a simple question. When a teacher asks you a 'yes' and 'no' question, you can't ever answer yes or no. Because the truth is, they are not interested in your answer, they are interested in your French. So when presented with a question that is asking your opinion, you are not only expected to answer, but give your reasons for that answer.

'No,' I responded, 'it's boring'. Then, thinking I should add a bit more I said, 'I prefer Picasso'.

All of a sudden Yann's face fell and his cheery demeanor went with it. He stared at me blankly for what seemed like minutes. At first I thought I must have said something wrong. Or offensive. Then I began to get that feeling you get when a guy is looking at you and you just know by the glazing over of his eyes that he's been lured deep into his mind, where sexual images are playing out and you are the star. Then he spoke.

'If you meet Patrick Bruel', he said intensely, in a low, slow voice, 'you must make sure you say Picasso'. There were a couple of seconds of silence, then Yann shook himself and became the old Yann again. It was totally unexpected and, I have to say, more than a little disturbing. Apparently there was just something about the way I said Picasso.

Part Three:
Advanced

Chapter 18
Margie faces her fear of Paris

At the restaurant

J'ai une réservation au nom de …

I have a reservation in the name of …

C'est un restaurant cher.

That is an expensive restaurant.

Je vais prendre …

I am going to have …

Quelle est la spécialité de la maison?

What is the house specialty?

Avez-vous des plats végétariens?

Do you have vegetarian dishes?

Avez-vous un menu?

Do you have a menu?

Qu'est-ce que vous suggérez?

What do you suggest?

Bon appétit!

'I'll have the children cutlets and worm salad with a palm tree, *s'il vous plâit*'. That's what I was dying to say, but the heavy build and impatient expression of the waiter caused Mum and me to rethink mocking the strange English translations on the menu. Instead, I pointed and smiled and sat back in my chair and watched the Parisian people bustling down Rue du Rivoli.

With Barry at the bar conference every day and Liz having to go to work, Mum and I spent our days wandering around the Paris shops and sitting in restaurants. Mum laughingly referred to it as 'research'. While she understood that I needed to visit these places for the articles I was writing, she did have trouble calling it 'work'. Just like she continued to refer to the DVDs, books and cosmetics I brought home from work as 'presents' rather than 'items for reviews'.

I was staying with Liz at her apartment in the fifteenth arrondissement. Every morning I caught the Metro to Mum's hotel in the first and we would spend the day together. While I loved Paris—the vibe, the sounds, the smells—it also rather frightened me. Being alone, even for small amounts of time, in a city where you rarely understand anything being said and you struggle to make yourself understood is scary. Every place looks foreign and you often don't know exactly where you are. You have to deal with bums in the street and aggressive advances from strange men, which is a new experience. Plus, I knew from the Millennium Eve trip that Parisians could be prone to random acts of violence.

While I was desperate to love Paris, every time I had been there in the past had been an experience of absolute joy—and apprehension. Being with Mum during the day meant that I was never really alone, except for the trip from Liz's house to her hotel. Liz wrote the route on a piece of paper for me—catch a train on line 6 (the green line) in the direction of Charles de Gaulle Étoile, change at Charles de Gaulle Étoile to line 1 (the yellow line) in the direction of Château de Vincennes, and get off at Tuileries. The whole journey took only around 20 minutes. They were lines that were heavily used, so I was always surrounded by people. Being summer it was tourist season and because Liz was right next to the Eiffel Tower and Mum was staying opposite the Louvre, there were always tourists on the train looking far more out of place and vulnerable than I.

Mum's hotel was directly opposite the Metro station on Rue du Rivoli and the only potential hiccup was crossing the very busy road. I soon discovered though, that about 100 metres up the road there was a set of lights, and it was no bother to walk up to the lights, cross, and walk back—certainly it was a lot less stressful than just marching across the road, hoping that the cars would stop as many Parisians did.

It made me feel more at home and less of a foreigner watching other foreigners sitting at the ridiculously overpriced restaurants along Rue de Rivoli. With their cameras and their high school French I could feel their anxiety and it pleased me to think I might not be quite at home but at least I am not like them.

At least I knew a rip-off restaurant when I saw one. Just once did Mum and I stop at one of these restaurants, and it was simply because we were hot, starving and thirsty. Plus, I thought, it would be good for my research. And in fact, it was very pleasant sitting in the sun, looking at all the great landmarks of Paris.

Our sidewalk cafe bliss evaporated when the waiter flung my meal onto the table, grunting in French a commentary about how Americans are uncultured. I stared down at the soggy, boiled carrots and peas, as the greasy gravy slid off the meat to reveal a rubbery piece of flesh, which had as much fat as meat.

In actuality, my 'research' into French food was teaching me a lot. French food is very often crap. My assumption that 'children' meant lamb (kids?) and that 'worm' should have read warm proved correct, although I have a suspicion that the temperature had been caused by the lettuce leaves sitting in a steaming bain marie for a couple of days.

When I complained to Liz about the appalling state of French food, she had to agree with me. As a vegetarian living in Paris, she had a lot to say about French eateries and none of it was good. She advised that I eat in restaurants not brasseries. Brasseries, she explained, tend to cater for foreign tourists who like to think they're eating authentic French food but still have the option of ordering hotdogs. This food is treated with the disdain reflected in the way Parisians treat tourists in general.

Your chances of getting a decent meal improve if you know what to order, she explained. The Parisians have a deep respect for seafood and most restaurants serve excellent quality shellfish dishes like mussels in white wine or garlic butter. Bread at the time was experiencing a renaissance, and I found there were many varieties of soda bread to order. Mushrooms are a national obsession and there are many varieties. Vegetarians can order *gratin*, a vegetable dish that can be eaten as a main.

Ten years earlier, when Liz was doing her exchange with a family in the south of France, I stayed with her and got my first dose of French home cooking. Michel, the patriarch, invited me to eat with the family and made it his mission to prove to me that French food is supreme.

Michel was a solid man with a bushy moustache atop a very serious expression, a chest that seemed permanently puffed out in pride, and a tendency to deliver slaps on the back with enough power to send you flying across the room. He was also very proud of his food. 'Is this acceptable?' he muttered as he entered the room holding up a chicken carcass by its feet, its neck dangling as he walked.

'*Bien*', I smiled, trying to conceal my horror.

Dinner at Michel's place always consisted of several *plats*. There was always a pasta, dressed in olive oil and garlic, a green salad, crusty bread and butter and some form of meat, usually roasted in herbs, wine and vegetables, and garlic. After the meal there was the obligatory cheese selection just in case there's a centimetre of your stomach that isn't stretched to bursting point.

I was beginning to realise that if you wanted to be sure of a decent meal in Paris, you have to make it yourself. Which would be fine, if the kitchens of Paris apartments were bigger than a broom closest. But in most cases they are not. On the rare night Liz and I ate at home, the meal consisted of bread and dips, a lightly dressed salad and an array of *charcuterie* and *saucisson* (sausages and preserved meats).

One morning, walking to the Metro Dupleix on my way to Mum's hotel, I turned the corner and for a moment had that punch in the stomach feeling that I was lost. The barren stretch of concrete beneath the railway tracks that's normally full of homeless people and a lot of rubbish had been transformed overnight into a colourful crowded food market, alive with people. It smelled divine.

There are 57 *marchés alimentaires* (fresh food markets) that spring up once or twice a week in Paris. I wandered down towards the Metro, passing stalls full of plump, firm vegetables, tables of offal, cheese, nuts, bread and strange animal parts like pigs' heads and trays of trotters. To the hungry, half-asleep tourist, it was a godsend. I bought a bag of warm nuts and was given a bunch of beautiful lilacs by the vendor, who must have sensed my appreciation.

Yet I quickly discovered that the most satisfying and tasty food a girl can eat in Paris doesn't come from a restaurant or market. Dotted along most of the main *Rues* in Paris are street vendors who whip up fresh crepes with the speed and agility of one who has done it all one's life. They coat the crepes in Nutella, jam or lemon and sugar, and wrap them in paper. So deliciously decadant are the crepes, that on a couple of occasions Mum and I walked down the Champs-Élysées with melted Nutella all over ours faces and hands and we didn't even care.

Chapter 19
Margie develops a Paris Personality

The passive form

Active: *Les étudiants organisent une fête.*

       The students organise a party.

Passive: *Une fête est organisée par les étudiants.*

       A party is organised by the students.

Active: *Les enfants feront la gâteu.*

       The children will make the cake.

Passive: *La gâteu sera fait par les enfants.*

       The cake will be made by the children.

The rudeness of the Parisians is the stuff that legends are made of. Their is no group of people that are more well known for their grumpiness than French waiters.

When Butterfly Butcher heard I was coming to Paris, she decided to come over from New York and visit for a weekend. Ian, one of Butterfly Butcher's colleagues from the New York office, who was French by birth, had been visiting his family and the plan was that when he arrived back in Paris, we'd all meet up and have lunch, and then the two of them would catch a taxi to the airport to go home. But as we were making our way to the restaurant, Ian called Butterfly Butcher on her mobile in a right state. He was already at the restaurant and he was being yelled at by the waiter.

As Butterfly Butcher tried to calm him down it became clear that Ian needed us to come *tout de suite*. He had taken a table at the designated eatery and had been waiting for ten minutes before the waiter demanded that he order or leave—he was holding valuable restaurant space.

In the time it took us to get to the Louvre, Butterfly Butcher received two more frantic calls about the screaming waiter. I could understand the waiter's frustration. It was peak tourist season and he was losing valuable custom.

Except he wasn't. When we arrived, panting from running down the street, we saw a relieved looking Ian—in a half-empty restaurant. The waiter barrelled up to us and threw menus in our direction. Because we were so late we only had fifteen minutes to eat and I was starving and in desperate need for a coffee. So I ordered a salad and a coffee.

'Mumble, mumble … *Américaines* … mumble', the waiter flung his hands up in the air and shook his head as he walked inside.

'What the hell's his problem?' I demanded.

'It's because you ordered a salad and a coffee,' Butterfly Butcher said with more than a little condescension, 'we don't do that in France'. Had she forgotten that she was in fact an Australian living in the United States who was spending the weekend in Paris?

According to Butterfly Butcher, Parisian waiters are the staunch defenders of traditional French dining. People wouldn't experience their wrath, if they just learnt the correct way to eat in a restaurant. It wasn't the first time I had heard this theory. The trouble is, I had never experienced it.

In order to avoid busloads of tourists, Mum, Barry and I frequented restaurants in the *arrondissement*, whose name literally translates as The Marsh. Le Marais is one of the oldest quarters of Paris, and the tiny, meandering streets and pre-revolution architecture make it a gorgeous area to explore. It's traditionally the Jewish area, although in the past decade it's become very trendy and is now considered to be the centre of gay life in Paris.

Le Chant des Voyelles (The Vowel Song) looked like any number of Paris restaurants, with its rows of cafe tables and chairs beneath a bright yellow canopy. Inside the restaurant, however, it was a scene from *The Birdcage* and our waiters were Robin Williams and Nathan Lane. They sang Vanessa Paradis (France's answer to Kylie Minogue) songs at the top of their voices and threw in a few flamboyant moves while managing to balance our two large plates of the most superbly cooked spicy couscous with vegetables.

They fawned over our clothes (you don't need a word of French to understand when a gay man is saying, '*Love* your handbag! *Where* did you get it?'), air-kissed every person who walked down the street, and managed to oh-so-casually plant themselves in the background of every single photo we took.

I was discovering that outrageous waiters are far more common than the fat, grumpy waiter of the stereotype. 'To see two beautiful girls laughing, it is a wonderful thing. The friendship!' exclaimed the stocky waiter in a small restaurant in the fifteenth, a regular haunt of Liz's, mainly because it doesn't turf you out when you order a dish *sans* meat.

Liz's response that we were actually sisters caused a little too much excitement for comfort. He stood there with a frozen smile on his face, giggling like a schoolgirl before we reminded him that he was actually supposed to be fetching our food. It was only when we got home that Liz discovered, nestled among the euros given to her as change, the waiter had slipped a note containing his name and phone number.

Then there was the handsome young waiter at Le Chien Qui Fume (The Smoking Dog), at Les Halles near Centre Pompidou, who insisted on having his photo taken with me. When we stood side-by-side he grabbed my backside and encouraged Mum to take more shots.

And Eric, the sprightly young waiter who performed at La Poule au Pot, just off Place de la Concorde, who laughed and flirted his way through dinner, and then handed us an autographed photo of himself as we left.

The truth is that the vast majority of Parisian waiters are friendly and welcoming, and immensely proud of their jobs. Unlike Australia, where waiters are normally students who would rather be at home piercing various body parts, waiters in France are older and normally male, to whom waiting on tables is a profession.

Butterfly Butcher was wrong about the ordering in France being the reason for the waiter's bad attitude. We should have expected a waiter with a bad attitude, considering we were in the heart of tourist Paris.

But it had nothing to do with what I ordered. He was giving tourists what was expected of the stereotype. You can order anything you like. It's the tourists who think you can't.

Trying to speak French in France was completely different from trying to speak French in class. In class, the teacher speaks to you at the level they know you are at. They use words, the most of which they know you understand. And most notably, they speak slowly and articulately. In France, they just speak to you and expect you to understand.

I knew from our Millennium Eve trip that speaking French in France required a lot of confidence. But I was discovering that in Paris, confidence is something that is essential to getting through the day.

If you don't stand up for yourself, Paris can be an enormously difficult city to be in. Let someone pass you in the Metro or on the street and they will quite literally push you to the ground on their way. Refuse to jostle into line to by a ticket and you'll still be there hours later, battered and bruised from all the elbowing. Stop to give a homeless person change and their accomplice will rip the purse out of your hand.

What I had learnt from being thrown against the magazine rack by a man during our Millennium Eve trip was that in Paris aggression is mainstream. It was not how I wanted to see Paris, but it was the reality. It's a rare trip on the Metro when you don't encounter a yelling match between two people, who may or may not know each other. And you never encounter someone waiting for their train with a smile or even a serene look on their face.

Parisians live under enormous pressure. They often live in cramped conditions, the streets are crowded and most people's wages are spent simply on existing. You can see the stress on their faces and in the way they behave towards each other.

In many cities in the world people live in extreme conditions. In Paris, the difference is that when people are angry, irritated or rushed, they let you know about it. My personality could not be further from that. I had just never liked to complain. Maeve, my former colleague at gURLpool, would say I never liked to stand up for myself, but whatever it was, I just did not enjoy the aggravation.

I had always been that way. When I was four my parents took me, my older brother Geoff, and my little brother Richard, on a walking tour of New Zealand. My parents aren't hugely athletic and for that reason, and perhaps also because Richard was strapped to my parents' backs, it wasn't a strenuous walk. But for children it was a huge effort.

According to my mother, it was hard to get Geoff, who was then about seven, to shut up. 'I want an orange!', 'I need to sit down!' and 'I want a drink!' was the soundtrack to the journey.

Towards the end of a day, Geoff was complaining that his feet hurt, so my parents decided to call it a day. I sat down on a rock, while Mum took off my shoes. She gasped in horror. My feet were swollen and covered in blisters and my socks were soaked in blood from where blisters had burst and my shoes had worn through to the skin beneath.

I must have been in excruciating pain—but I just kept on walking without saying a word. Mum says she yelled at me until I started to cry, and then took the approach she thought would be more effective: she tried to encourage me to speak up when I had had enough or was in pain. But I never did, and she spent my entire childhood worried about my wellbeing.

She had good reason to be worried, too. I had suffered from dreadful asthma as a child and there were many late night emergency dashes to the hospital. Mum says that many times she would come into my room and find me gasping for breath. I had obviously been that way for some time, but to her frustration I never let her know.

One night my mother came home late from work. I was still in primary school. She came in to my room to say goodnight and as she recalls, I was blue in the face and barely breathing. She immediately called an ambulance and I was rushed to hospital. 'Why?' she half-cried and half-yelled at me when they had attached me to oxygen and my breathing was beginning to return to normal.

'Why in God's name didn't you tell your father you were having an asthma attack?'

'I did', I apparently replied. 'He told me to be a good girl and go back to bed.'

So, screaming at Parisians in the street was not something that came naturally. If someone pushed ~~passed~~ ^past^ me or if a bum hassled me in the street it was just easier to ignore it and hope that it passed. Not having the language to scream back didn't help. But it was humiliating to just stand there and take abuse, and it made me feel vulnerable—as though I was sending a strong message to everyone that you could take your best shot at me and I would do nothing.

One morning on the Metro, I stood amongst commuters on their way to work wearing the same blank expression as my fellow travellers. Two drunk derros got on at the other end of the carriage. They were middle-aged and looked as though they had spent a good part of those years on the streets. They were filthy and offensive. They walked through the carriage confronting people and demanding money. At least, that's what I assumed. They spoke rapidly with drunken slurs, so I couldn't understand what they were saying. Some people ignored them, a couple of men gave them change. Whether they were yelling abuse or thanking people, they gesticulated wildly and yelled.

My chest tightened. I just knew what was going to happen. They would see me. Pretty, young, vulnerable in appearance and they would think it was Christmas. They would demand money and when I ignored them, they would abuse and humiliate me. And what could I do? I couldn't understand them so I couldn't respond to them with words.

Gripping onto the rail to brace myself, the men shuffled down the aisle and one of them looked at me. As he approached I creased my brow and frowned. In desperation as he got closer I 'tsked' and slowly waved a finger at him—like a teacher might do to a naughty child.

The man immediately looked down to the ground and kept walking. He looked ashamed. I was shocked at the power of such a small action. I didn't even need to speak. My expression spoke a thousand words.

The station was crowded. As I made my way up the stairs a woman carrying a large shopping bag stopped suddenly in front of me, looking at the street signs. I had to slam on my brakes and almost ran into the back of her. In annoyance, I adopted an irritated expression. For added effect I foofed.

The woman with the bag wasn't looking, but other people were. A very elegant older woman wearing an immaculately placed scarf caught my eye, frowned and nodded, as if to say, 'Yes, there are bloody idiots on the Metro'. I nodded knowingly and kept walking.

I began to freely use expressions to display my irritation, anger or even happiness. While I stopped short of screaming at strangers standing in my way, I found myself elbowing my way through crowds, frowning aggressively at unruly behaviour, and tsk-ing when someone annoyed me. Rather than being constantly on guard and maintaining a blank expression, I simply acted out what I was feeling with confidence. And it was strangely liberating. Once I began freely expressing emotions as I felt them, I began to relax. I realised that so much of my life was spent hiding what I really felt for the sake of keeping the peace.

What I noticed, though, was that the Paris Personality takes a while to rub off. It can be quite helpful in getting you what you want (Australians are so unused to aggression) but can also have your friends wondering how one can be so uptight after a month-long holiday.

The sun was shining brightly one morning, so I decided to ditch the Metro and walk to Mum's hotel instead. I was wearing black Capri pants, a plain white shirt and I had a scarf tied around my neck. Plus, I had my newfound Paris accessory: the Paris Personality—a mixture of pride and indifference.

Even though it had just turned 8am, the tourist buses were already beginning to pull up alongside the Eiffel Tower and American tourists in their shorts and polo shirts spilled out onto the street with cameras dangling from their necks.

I was aware that a middle-aged man was staring at me and as I approached he said within earshot, 'You see, honey. That's a real French woman'. He seemed very proud of his observation.

'Actually, I am Australian,' I smiled as I passed him, 'and you should be careful. Most people in Paris speak English'. The man looked shocked and his teenage kids sniggered.

I was pleased with myself for my response and more than a little thrilled that he had mistaken me for a 'real French woman'. I can't wait to tell Mum, I thought. On reflection though, I realised Mum probably wouldn't think anything of it. Neither would Ky. I picked up my mobile and punched in Julie's number.

'*Bienvenue à Paris!*' she answered the phone.

I recounted the story of what had just passed and Julie could only have been happier if it had happened to her. 'Margie,' she gushed, 'it is true; we *are* French women!'

Chapter 20
Stepping back in time in Paris

Hypothesise using the word 'if'

Si + présent + futur

Si j'obtiens une augmentation de salaire, nous déménagerons.

If I get a raise, we will move.

Si + imparfait + conditionnel passé

Si j'étais riche, j'aurais pu acheter les vêtements qui me plaisent.

If I was rich, I would have been able to buy the clothes that
I like.

Si + plus que parfait + conditionnel passé

S'il avait gagné le gros lot, il n'habiterait plus dans ce petit studio.

If he had won the jackpot, he would not live in this small studio
anymore.

'There will be a lot of screaming,' a journalist friend of Liz warned me
on the way to the Patrick Bruel's Paris concert, 'but don't worry, they're
not screaming at you'. He was being funny, but not that funny. Patrick
Bruel is one of Europe's best-loved and enduring sex symbols. I was
fully prepared for a whole lot of teenage screaming and panty throwing.
While I've never felt the desire to propel my underwear at musicians, I
had been a teenager once. Hey, I went to a Duran Duran concert at the
height of their success—I knew exactly what a Patrick Bruel concert
would be like.

I didn't. The only screaming happened when Bruel first appeared on
stage and that only lasted about a minute. The rest of the night the

audience spent with their arms linked, swaying side by side and singing tunes from the 1930s.

This was Paris in 2002, a place where conservative politics had reached frightening popularity and where teenage girls knew the words to songs their grandparents sang in the years between the world wars. Where a pop star responsible for the outpouring of adoration labelled 'Bruelmania' by the media dumped his image to sing about the good old days, which, at the age of forty-three, he wasn't even old enough to remember.

Patrick Bruel first came to my attention during our Millennium Eve European trip, while we were spending a few days in Nice. After Millennium Eve, Aussie Bogan and British Bogan had returned to England, and Ky, Freda and I headed down to Barcelona. My mum, who was holidaying at her house in Ireland, flew to Spain to meet up with us and spend a few days in Barcelona and then the south of France.

Mum, Ky and I were getting along fine, but cracks were beginning to appear in the Ky and Freda relationship. They didn't have an existing friendship, they only knew of each other through me, and by this stage Freda was getting tired of travelling and was wanting the trip to be over so she could return home to her much-missed boyfriend. Ky, being so sweet and amiable, was becoming a frequent target of Freda's outbursts, partly because they had to share a room while Mum and I shared the other and partly because Ky just took it.

After spending the day walking around Nice we had gone back to the hotel to rest and change before going out to dinner. When I was dressed, I decided to go next door and see how the girls were doing. I thought it was odd that the only sound I could hear coming from their room was the television. No talking or laughter or movement. The door was ajar, so I just walked in.

Freda and Ky were sitting side by side on the end of one of the beds, staring at the television screen with expressions that would have been blank except for the gaping mouths.

'Hi', I said warily.

'Margie, have a look at this', said Ky, without turning away from the television. I looked. They were watching an interview with a dark, handsome, softly spoken man. What was amazing was that Ky and Freda were hanging on every word he said—and neither had a word of French. They were just captivated by his voice and his beauty.

Of course at that stage my comprehension was practically non-existent, so I wasn't any help. The best I could do was offer a word here and there.

'He's talking about his father', I said after a while.

'Ahhh', nodded Freda. 'That's a difficult relationship ...' It's amazing what you can understand when you don't comprehend the spoken word.

The next day we all went out and bought Patrick Bruel's latest CD *Juste Avant* and spent the rest of the trip sighing whenever we listened to it. And now, two years later, I was going to see the man in person.

During my email correspondence with the BMG publicist Valérie, it became apparent that a face-to-face interview with Bruel was going to be impossible. Bruel's CD was selling out fast and he was having to add more and more concerts to the schedule to meet the demand. But they would give me tickets to the first show, which would provide me with enough information to write an article on, so I was more than happy.

The publicist at BMG left a message on Liz's phone saying I should stop in and pick up the tickets from the BMG office in the eighth. It was a particularly hot day and after a long morning of 'research', Mum decided to go back to her hotel for a sleep while I went to BMG.

The record company office wasn't hard to find and was in walking distance from the hotel. Although situated in an old building in the financial district, inside it was all modern and funky. Gold records and posters of their artists hung on the walls and music blared from hidden speakers. While the girls on reception looked like punk rockers, BMG was the model of professionalism. Valérie came down and gave me the tickets and organised for the CD and numerous press-clippings to be couriered to Liz's apartment.

The concert tour came on the heels of Patrick Bruel's new CD *Entre Deux,* which meant Between Two, and referred to the period between world wars. It was a collection of beautiful vintage French songs that were dripping with sentimentality and nostalgia.

The Paris concert itself was a real step back in time, designed to make the audience believe they were patrons at a smoky Paris bar. The stage was a scene from a black and white movie, complete with street lamp, bar and tables and a cast of men and women twirling around a dance floor to the music. Patrick Bruel appeared wearing a baggy, old-style suit, until he changed into a waistcoat, a street urchin hat and cranked up a pianola. It could not have been a greater departure from what I had come to expect from Patrick Bruel.

Bruelmania really took off in the early nineties, thanks to the album *Alors Regarde*. When a concert tour was announced in the spring of 1991, 8000 tickets were sold in a matter of hours. *Alors Regarde* climbed the European and Canadian charts and his videos were then reproduced in several languages. By the end of the year the album had sold over two million copies and the tour was such a success that BMG released a live CD that sold around a million.

Rather than developing a migraine from all the screaming, Bruel, by all appearances, lapped up the attention. His charm and flirtatious nature fuelled the fantasies of adolescent girls and in the nineties he was posing for too many pictures that scream 'Eurotrash' (think Miami Vice cotton blazers and pastel T-shirts) that must surely now make him cringe.

From what I could tell from conversations with Liz's colleagues at the embassy, a lot of people saw the theme of Bruel's latest venture as a reflection of an illness currently gripping French society. Whilst the success of ultra-right winged conservative politician Jean-Marie Le Pen in the presidential elections had led to nationwide protests and the ultimate re-election of Chirac, it was a frightening demonstration of the growth in popularity of the Right. Some saw Bruel's shameless nostalgia for the past as feeding the public's desire for a return to traditional values, and the fact that young people are embracing *Entre Deux* is scary, not quaint. The good old days, they say, were also the days of sexism, racism and hypocrisy.

Yet according to the clippings, Patrick Bruel had vocally opposed the Right for years and claimed that *Entre Deux* is more about hope and optimism, reflecting the celebration of peace during the period between wars. Leaving the Paris Casino the night of the concert I wasn't concerned. I was baffled, yes, impressed greatly, and when I debriefed the French journalist who had warned me about the screaming, he didn't scoff or crack any Patrick Bruel jokes. He went out and bought the CD.

Chapter 21
Drinking champagne—there is a right way and a wrong way

Colloquialisms: drinking

Arroser un évènement	To celebrate by drinking
Avoir un coup dans l'aile/être pompette	To be tipsy
Se soûler la gueule	To get smashed
Être une éponge	To drink like a fish
Avoir la gueule de bois	To have a hangover

All the time I was in Paris I was collecting story ideas for future articles and one destination I knew I wouldn't have any trouble pitching to editors was Champagne.

There's something about champagne that is synonymous with glamour and style. It has toasted millions of weddings and births, promotions and windfalls; it has launched a thousand ships and attended the world's most glamorous parties. It's a drop synonymous with joy and festivity. It's a wine that is universally recognised as so much more special than the others are and with good reason. From its glamorous history, to making it and all the occasions it helps celebrate, champagne is special.

During one of the weekends we spent in Paris, Liz, Mum, Barry and I took the train out to the champagne-making capital of the world. As soon as you step off the train at Eperney you know you are in a very special village. To begin with, everything is so clean and neat. The gardens are perfectly manicured and bursting with colour, the stores are cute to the point that they almost don't look real and the people are polite and very quiet.

Epernay, which is around an hour's train journey from Paris, is where the serious business of making champagne takes place, but Epernay is also very accommodating to the tourist.

Our first stop was the tourist information building, located at the foot of Avenue de Champagne, the only street in Epernay you need to know. The avenue houses one famous *maison de champagne* after another. The houses, most of which are nineteenth century in classical or neo-renaissance architecture, stand proudly above the cellars—said to hold more than ninety million bottles.

All the maisons de champagne conduct guided tours for a small price, and provide you with a flute to taste afterwards. Every house has a unique story to tell, we were told at Tourist Information, so it's worth visiting more than one. The larger houses, like Mercier, have organised tours of the underground caves in trains.

We started our tour at the one place I had to go—Moët & Chandon. The house is immaculately maintained, surrounded by a black and brass fence with the name displayed in regal-looking letters. The tour of the house began with a short video explaining the champagne-making process, as well as some of the colourful history.

The godlike mystique surrounding champagne has its roots in the very creation of the drink. Dom Pérignon, who is said to have been one of the original makers of champagne, was a monk who lived at the Benedictine Abbey of Hautvillers, just outside Epernay, in the heart of the Champagne district of France. Being a man of God, he spent his spare time praying—praying that too many champagne bottles in his cellar wouldn't burst. Although he had the vision, his practical skills were somewhat lacking and documents of the time tell of the endless sounds of explosions coming from the abbey's cellar.

The French royals and aristocracy have always taken champagne very seriously. In 1729, a year after Ruinart became the first recorded Champagne house, King Louis XV issued a royal ordinance dictating the size, shape and weight of champagne bottles, the size of the cork that should be used and ordered that they be secured with strong pack thread to the neck of the bottle.

Napoleon may have been short on stature but history tells us he was big on taste. His special relationship with champagne enhanced the legend. The great leader would stop at Epernay to visit his friend, Jean-Rémy Moët and celebrate his victories with a few barrels of bubbly. In fact, Moët & Chandon Brut Impérial was created in his honour.

Champagne is also the stuff of modern-day heroes. For more than four decades Agent 007 Bond has been shamelessly enjoying his Bollinger Champagne. In the 1995 film *Golden Eye* (the seventh in which Bollinger has been featured), Bond, played by Pierce Brosnan, is asked what he does for relaxation by a female psychiatrist sent to evaluate him. In response, Bond presses a button on his Aston Martin's dashboard to reveal a secret refrigerated compartment containing a bottle of Bollinger Grande Annee 1988 and two glasses.

Like A-list movie stars, champagne also features regularly at glamorous premieres and film festivals. Piper-Heidsieck is the official champagne of the festivals in Cannes and Deauville, as well as the Sundance Film Festival. Piper-Heidsieck is also the champagne of major film award ceremonies, including the Oscars and the Césars.

Our tour ended with a glass of champagne. We'd already seen that there is a lot more to making champagne than we imagined, so it was no surprise that there's a whole lot more to drinking it, which we were about to learn.

Between downing glasses of champagne, I spent the day furiously scribbling notes. And not just for the article. Julie had left me with strict instructions that in order to be Real French Women, it was essential that we drink champagne—'The stuff that comes from France, Margie, not the other stuff.' Shudder. It was also important we drink it the correct way—'The only way, Margie. Like the French.'

Champagne can be stored at home, but only for the same length of time it was aged at the champagne house. Conditions must be a cool temperature and light is not permitted. Champagne bottles must be stored horizontally to keep the cork moist. This will keep the gas in and the air out. Champagne should be served in long-stemmed flutes or tulip-shaped glasses. These are designed to enhance the flow of bubbles and to concentrate the aromas of the wine. In a perfect world it would be served in crystal because the surface texture of crystal is rougher than ordinary glass, and more bubbles form in these glasses.

Some people will tell you that the only way to drink champagne is from a champagne coupe or saucer-shaped glass. They're lying. There is a legend that it was modelled from the bosom of Marie-Antoinette, but as quaint (and strangely disturbing) as that story is, the bubbles and the aroma are all over the place.

Champagne is best served cold at about 7°C, a temperature that enables the smell and taste to be fully appreciated. This temperature can be achieved by placing the unopened bottle in an ice bucket (filled with half ice and half water) for 30 minutes. Alternatively, you can refrigerate it for three hours, but never longer. Never place it in the freezer.

Only remove enough of the foil to be able to loosen or remove the twisted-wire hood. Hold the bottle away from you and anyone else (resist the temptation!) at a 45° angle. Champagne is precious stuff, so place the mouth of the bottle nearest to the first champagne glass to be filled in case it begins to gush out of the bottle. Hold the cork and gently turn the bottle (not the cork—they tell me this is important) in one direction.

Be careful that the cork does not pop. There's a saying that goes, 'The ear's gain is the palate's loss'. In practical terms, it just means you waste bubbles when you pop the cork. When properly executed it should come off with a quiet sigh. Like a kiss.

Before pouring, the neck should be wiped with a clean linen napkin. Then begin by pouring about three centimetres into everyone's glass allowing the froth to settle. Then, top up to about two-thirds full. This will prevent any frothing over.

In cases of emergency, you can save champagne once it has been opened (because surely only a life and death situation would prevent you from polishing off the entire bottle). If it has been closed using a champagne stopper and placed in a refrigerator, it should be good for another several days. Dangling the handle of a silver spoon in the neck of the bottle will keep the wine sparkling for a few hours.

Who knew there was so much involved in drinking bubbly?

The pace of the trip began to take its toll on Mum. By lunchtime the next day she was tired after a morning of shopping and wanted to have a rest at her hotel. I still had a couple of shopping centres I needed to visit to take photos for my fashion article, so I dropped her at her hotel and walked up to the shopping district of l'Opéra. I returned a couple of hours later and plonked myself on the bed next to her.

I told her about my visit to Galleries Lafayette and that the public relations manager had shown me through all the latest merchandise. 'Can you believe', I asked, rolling over to face her, 'in that whole store, I couldn't find one thing I wanted to buy?'

Mum stared at me for a moment and then said, 'Margie, I am so proud of you'.

'Well, it wasn't for want of trying,' I laughed. 'I did actually want to buy *something!*'

'No, I just can't believe how well you have nailed this town', she said. 'You're zipping around the place, meeting with all these people you have never met before, having no problem at all with the language ...'

'Mum,' I said, 'I am having heaps of problems with the language'.

'If you are, then you're not letting it stop you. You're not the slightest bit intimidated.'

I had been so busy running around collecting information in France that I hadn't stopped to realise that I wasn't worried about getting around by myself any more.

Chapter 22
French takes a nasty turn

You: plural and formal usage

Do you have a pen?
As-tu un stylo? (singular)
Avez-vous un stylo? (plural/formal)

Do you know that film?
Connais-tu ce film? (singular)
Connaissez-vous ce film? (plural/formal)

Did you wear a dress?
As-tu porté une robe? (singular)
Avez-vous porté une robe? (plural/formal)

Because I was overseas in the middle of the year, it was unavoidable that I would miss the first three lessons of one semester. While I was in Paris, Julie texted me and filled me in on our new French teacher. He was from Paris, she wrote, and he was very handsome. While I was excited about the prospect, I didn't quite believe it. Partly because I was aware the Julie was desperate to meet a handsome French man with whom to embark on the romance of a lifetime, but mainly because while there's the myth of the dashing French man, the sad truth is that in France the pickings are pretty slim.

Julie frequently talked about French men as if they were the sexiest men on the planet. She had only been to Paris once and that was five years before. I don't know where she saw these godlike creatures, but they certainly weren't frequenting the places I was going.

We Australians have been spoiled by our bronzed, athletic males and the French men—pale and insipid by comparison—don't stand a chance. Except for one exception—*les pompiers*. Firemen in Paris are so much more than firemen. They are the heroes of Paris. They can put out fires, naturally, but they can also administer first aid and beat up the bad guys. If you want the law administered you call the police, but if you want a man to save you, you call the *pompiers*.

Pompiers are highly trained professionals; another obvious requirement for the *pompiers* is that they be built. The bodies of the *pompiers* are emphasised by their uniforms—tight pants, high boots and muscle T-shirts. It's enough to make a girl set fire to her apartment. Luckily, Liz lived across the road from a housing commission building, to which the *pompiers* were frequently called. We spent many an evening hanging out the window watching the *pompiers* at work.

For those who are unfortunate enough to live in a wealthy neighbourhood, or a particularly fire-retardant building, the Paris policemen also make a satisfactory perv. They may not be as built, but they do wear hot Thunderbird uniforms and they have huge, semi-automatic weapons strapped to their person. In Paris, many policemen get around on rollerblades (let's face it, they'd never get to a crime scene if they had to make their way through Paris traffic), and sometimes jumping in front of one can suddenly seem a sane and rational thing to do.

Yet Yves was a teacher, not a *pompier,* so when Julie texted me and said that he was handsome, I did wonder if he really was or if Julie's desire for a French man wasn't clouding her judgment. Although, while I was in Europe, Julie and I spoke on the phone every couple of days and I had noticed that conversation about Laurant had diminished. In one conversation, she hadn't even mentioned him. 'How's Laurant?' I finally asked.

'Good. You know.'

'Is he still writing to you?'

'Yep.' That was it.

When she picked me up for French, I pushed a little more. 'What's going on with Laurant?'

Julie looked a little sad. 'Nothing really', she said. 'He's still great and everything, but ... Margie, in every single letter he says he has gone out on a date! I don't get it! Do you think he could be a bastard?'

'With the same girl?'

'He doesn't say! All he ever says is that he went on a date! But it's every week and it's every Sunday night.'

'Man', I said. 'Maybe he is a player, I don't know. Listen Jules, you're not going to know until you get there. I don't think we should guess at what's going on, because we'll probably be wrong.'

'Anyway', said Julie, perking up, 'wait 'til you see Yves!'

There is something really unattractive about the way French men laugh. The older, fatter ones are excluded from this generalisation because they tend to have deep-belly booming laughs. It's the younger ones, in particular the young Parisians, who have the problem. Quite simply, they laugh like girls, with silly, high-pitched giggles that they have absolutely no control over and which subsequently contain more than a few snorts. The actions that go with laughter make it worse. They will stare at you with wide eyes and a foolish smile on their faces while nodding frantically.

Yves laughed like this, but because he was handsome we let it pass. Julie had told me that he was hot and it actually turned out to be true, which was a surprise, because although we remained optimistic, no hot guys had ever crossed our paths at the Alliance.

Dressed in a roll neck jumper and jeans and wearing round glasses, Yves looked like a French intellectual. Maybe he was slightly thin for my tastes and his hair did go a bit boofy when it got too long, but he was the closest thing we had ever got to a babe at the Alliance.

I had my speech prepared and when he opened the classroom door I launched into it. 'My name's Margaret Ambrose', I said in French. 'I am enrolled in this class but I have been in Paris ...'

'Yes, I have been expecting you.' He smiled. 'Come in and can you please stay back after class?'

Could I ever! Julie and I looked at four total strangers and a teacher who was new to us and I realised that for the first time, we were the freaks, the newies that had come into the tight-knit group at the beginning of every semester. Worse still, there weren't two seats free next to each other.

'Excuse me', I said to a middle-aged Sri Lankan man. 'Would you mind moving up one?' He looked at me as if I was asking him to give me his first born and started stuttering something about having all his books laid out just so.

Thankfully, my Paris Personality hadn't yet worn off. 'For God's sake, I'm just asking you to move up one seat!' I exclaimed. Yves said something to him and passed him a chair. I'm not sure why the man was upset, maybe he was particularly attached to the chair—who knows? We were, however, very impressed that Yves understood the importance of Julie and I sitting together.

On the upside, Miranda and Fräulein hadn't continued with their classes. That was a good sign, I thought, maybe this will be a fun class, like our classes used to be.

After class, Julie and I stayed back to speak to Yves. He handed me some French articles that the class had been studying and explained what sort of things we would be studying in the classes to come. His pronunciation of English was poor and his vocab not very extensive. But that's cute, I told myself.

'We weel bee doing a lot of conversations', he explained. I nodded with a smile on my face, even though my heart was sinking. I no longer struggled with grammar, verb conjugations or sentence structure, but I still had trouble understanding the spoken language. I knew I lacked the confidence needed to express myself verbally. Still, I thought, practising conversation is the only way to overcome this.

'You are not very good at speaking', continued Yves, with a deadpan expression, 'so you must do a lot of this in the class'.

I was gobsmacked. Could this guy read my mind? Soon, surprise was replaced by indignation. 'What?' I demanded. 'How would you know how good my speaking is after one lesson?'

Yves stared at me blankly.

'Just so you know,' I continued, 'my speaking improved tremendously when I was in France'.

Still no expression from Yves.

'Plus, I am very tired', I continued, although at this point I was beginning to wonder how I was going to be able to stop this diatribe.

I didn't need to, though, because Julie stepped in.

'Margie', she said urgently. 'He didn't mean *you* as in you personally, he meant "you" as in the whole class!'

The irony was, if Yves had been speaking in French I would have understood him better. While in English 'you' can mean the individual or collective, the French have two words: 'tu' which means you alone, and 'vous' which means a whole group of you.

We may have gotten off to a rocky start, but it wasn't long before we started to feel sorry for Nigel, the Sri Lankan man. His French was shocking. There was always a ten-second pause between words when he spoke, and the words were usually wrong. He reminded us of how we were in the Intermediate classes with Aleksandra, except then everyone was the same level. In Advance everyone was good. His *confiance* was worse than ours. He blushed fiercely whenever he got a sentence wrong or couldn't understand what the teacher was saying. It was so painful to watch. No wonder he was so thrown by the suggestion that he move seat. Knowing where he was sitting every week was probably the only comforting thing for him in the entire class.

In the weeks that followed Nigel sat at the back of the room with Julie and I, facing the front. On one side was Tim, and on the other side was the girl who made the class a nightmare, Mary. Tim and Mary faced each other and while I am not certain, I was fairly convinced that every so often I saw exchanges of meaningful eye contact.

The vibe in the room was really tense and serious and I realised after about ten minutes in the class that my Paris Personality was going to serve me well. I wasn't the only one. Foofing Woman was in her late thirties and slightly rough looking. There was nothing unusual about her speech or the way she expressed herself. Yet, when the class started she transformed into a loud, expressive French woman who spoke in a way that suggested she was constantly angry. That is, like a Parisian.

The most obvious way this manifested itself was in foofing. The French have an action that is constantly used. They blow out a breath, filling up their jaw with air, which puffs out and makes a foofing noise. The French foof to show disapproval, annoyance or incredulity. It's an integral part of the Paris Personality.

Foofing Woman would foof at every opportunity and it drove Julie crazy. There's nothing a Francophile hates more than another Francophile who doesn't do it with style. In Julie's eyes, Foofing Woman was wasting her time foofing, because she wasn't French, would never be French, and should stop annoying everyone by trying.

In her defence, I can understand how once someone starts foofing it can be very difficult to stop. For such a little action it's very powerful. Foofing helped me get around Paris and when I left Paris I foofed through Ireland and Germany. When I got back to Australia I had to consciously control myself from foofing any more.

Overt expressions of anger and annoyance are considered very hostile in Australia. Soon after I returned, I was in a car park and the woman parked next to me opened her door and it slightly banged my car. I foofed and creased my brow and I was shocked at how apologetic the woman was. She thought I was really angry. She didn't understand the French subtleties of the foof.

Fräulein's threatening presence in the classroom paled in comparison to Mary. If you could relate Fraulein's aggressive and obnoxious personality to her lack of any physical beauty, perhaps Mary's worse attitude could be attributed to the fact that she wasn't just plain, she was unfortunate looking, with pale skin covered in huge freckles and out of control frizzy red hair.

While Fräulein concentrated her nastiness on Claire, she was only intolerant of the other class members. Mary, on the other hand, had an agenda that included humiliating and defeating every other student in the room. Mary reminded me of Bag Lady as she set out to establish herself as an intellectual bohemian. She would scoff at popular opinions and claimed she never read the newspaper because it wasn't intelligent.

Once, she asked Yves how to say, 'at work'. Yves replied, '*au travail*' (at work) or '*au bureau*' (at the office). Mary scoffed and with an indignant expression exclaimed, 'Well I couldn't say "*au bureau*"! As if I would work in an office!'

This comment was a double triumph for Mary because not only had she reinforced that she's not one of the masses that go to an office every day, she made everyone else in the class who did work in an office feel bad about it.

Most often the victim of Mary's venom was Nigel, because he made more errors than anyone else, and because he was so timid there would be no threat of a comeback. Plus, there was instant gratification because after a callous laugh or mocking correction from Mary, Nigel would look totally shattered and not say a word for the rest of the class.

Halfway through the semester, Julie found herself the target. Julie never blurted out a response to have it then corrected by the teacher. When she was asked a question she would think for a few seconds and then deliver a well thought out, grammatically correct response.

During one particular class, Mary decided she would take advantage of this pause. Every time Julie was asked a question Mary turned to her and said in the most condescending voice, 'That means ...' as though the reason Julie was pausing was because she didn't understand the question. Julie was miffed, but let it pass.

The next lesson I became the target. Advanced 1 concentrated on arguing—presenting an idea, forming an opinion and then explaining why you hold that opinion. At the end of every class, Yves handed out an article, which we read and translated as homework. We'd then spend the next class discussing the ideas in the article.

This article was about the Farm Bill, a piece of legislation passed by the United States government granting huge subsidies to their farmers. The subsidies meant farmers from the United States could sell their produce at dramatically reduced prices. The result was it was crippling the industries of other nations, including Australia.

We discussed the issues in class and then Yves asked us what animals threaten the livelihood of farmers. We discussed rabbits, cane toads, foxes—all introduced species. Then I said, 'Emus'. At the top of her voice, Mary said mockingly, 'Just between you and me, Margie, emus are native to Australia!' She burst out laughing and to my horror everyone else joined in, including Yves.

I was so angry I felt like the top of my head was going to explode. 'I am aware of that,' I snapped, 'but I thought we were talking about threats to farmers, not introduced species'.

She threw her head back laughing and said incredulously, 'Emus?'

'Actually, yes, emus are a big threat to farmers', contributed Yves.

'Emus?' Mary mocked. 'As if?'

'Yes, really', stressed Yves. 'It's been on the news in the past few weeks.'

Mary threw up her hands in exasperation. 'Whatever!' she exclaimed, as if she was suddenly bored by the conversation.

I didn't respond, because the words wouldn't come—even in English. I was not just humiliated. I was angry at myself for once again not speaking up against someone who had hurt me. The Paris Personality didn't extend that far. It was okay for expressing anger at someone who had done something against you, but not for articulating responses to someone who dismissed you as insignificant.

After a particularly nasty incident involving Nigel, we decided Mary had to be stopped. Julie and I decided we had to take action. The class had been divided up into two groups to play a game. Mary, Nigel and I were on one team. Julie, Tim and Foofing Woman were on the other. The game was a little like charades but with no actions. One team would be given a slip of paper with a word on it and they had to get the other team to guess what that word was, using sentences of less than three words. One time, for example, our word was *'sucre'* (sugar). The clues we gave were *'utilisé pour faire un gâteau'* (used in cakes), *'vient de canne'* (comes from cane), and *'blanc'* (white).

The other team's word was 'France', and the first clue they gave was, *'une pays'* (a country). In one of the rare instances Nigel actually spoke, he said thoughtfully, 'Well, it's something to do with finance I guess because "paye" sounds like "pay".'

Mary roared with laughter. She grabbed her sides and cried, 'Nigel! It means country!' She laughed at the top of her lungs for a good five minutes as Nigel went bright red and slunk down into his chair.

Naturally, Nigel said very little for the rest of the game, but that only provided Mary with more ammunition. 'Come on Nigel', she would cry mockingly. 'Give it a go; we know you can do it.' At which she would crack up all over again.

It was devastating to watch. I was a little angry that Yves didn't step in but I guess there wasn't much he could do. On the way home Julie and I discussed what had passed and that's when we decided we had to do something. We realised we couldn't actually plan a humiliation—we would have to wait until Mary slipped up and then pounce. But in the meantime we could at least stop her hurting Nigel. We decided that should she put him down we would simply turn and say, 'Is it absolutely necessary to be cruel?' Hopefully the embarrassment would be enough to get her to stop.

As it turns out, we didn't have to do anything. A substitute teacher we had for one of the classes did it all for us. Annibelle was a typical young, French beauty, sweet and fresh-faced. We spent the class reading extracts from books and comic strips and discussing what we thought about them. Mary was actually quite well behaved, perhaps because Nigel was absent, so Julie and I figured we had missed our opportunity for revenge.

At the end of the class, the teacher handed out an article Yves wanted us to read for homework. It was about the concept of beauty. It was an issue about which, herself being so unattractive, Mary had very strong views on.

We briefly read the first couple of paragraphs and the teacher explained what they meant. 'There was an experiment where many four-day-old babies were shown a picture of a beautiful woman and a picture of an ugly woman', she explained. 'And they all stared at the beautiful woman!'

'That's terrible,' exclaimed Mary, angrily. 'Four days old and they have already been brainwashed!'

'No, not brainwashed', began the teacher.

'Even an idiot knows that beauty is a made-up concept created by the media and big business to make money!' Mary continued indignantly.

Too bad for Mary she hadn't read the rest of the article. 'The scientists say', said the teacher, 'that things that make a woman beautiful are often health things'. Even worse for Mary was that the teacher had pretty bad English. 'People are attracted to beautiful people so they will mate and have healthy children. It's necessary for the continuation of the species that ugly people die out.'

Oblivious of what she had just done, the teacher started packing up her things. Mary looked like she was about to cry. Not only had she been humiliated in front of the class, she had just discovered that her appearance was a threat to the human race.

Chapter 23
The girls meet two hot French men

Job hunting

Un travail	A job
Les petites annonces	Classified ads
Emploi à temps plein	Full-time employment
Emploi à mi-temps	Part-time employment
L'agence de placement	Employment centre
Une demande d'emploi	Job application

Spending time in Europe had opened my eyes to a whole new world of work possibilities. For the first time I had travelled through Europe with work on my mind. I collected enough information to write articles for Australian publications as was my intention, but while I was in Europe I realised something else. There were English language magazines in every country that I visited. Why not pitch story ideas to them?

The more I thought about it the more the plan solidified. How great would it be to write for magazines at home as well as magazines in France! I could easily fit in a couple of visits a year, all the better if I could get paid for it. Spending time in France, meeting new people, my French would become perfect, I thought.

Thanks to the Internet I was able to find names and contact details of English language publications in France. I also contacted the editors of magazines in Ireland and the UK. I sent article pitches to every publication I could. As I expected, only a few even bothered to answer my emails, but the ones that did were very interested in my ideas, and over several months I managed to sell several articles I had collected while I was overseas.

Writing for French language magazines was out of the question. Even someone much more advanced than me would have difficulties writing in French. Just because English is your first language, it doesn't mean that you can automatically write publishable articles in English. Writing for magazines and newspapers is a very specific genre, with its own style, language and idioms. Journalists study and work for years to perfect their craft in English, never mind another language.

Through my Internet search I happened across the French equivalent of gURLpool. *Paris Woman Journal* was an online women's magazine edited with a very similar style—intelligent and sassy. When I contacted the editor, Juliette, she visited gURLpool and saw the similarity. Over the next few months, Juliette and I developed an email relationship. *Paris Woman Journal* was in its infancy and a lot of the difficulties Juliette was encountering were the same as gURLpool experienced at the beginning. I was able to offer Juliette a lot of good advice for which she was appreciative. I contributed several articles to *Paris Woman Journal,* and although it didn't pay very well, I had the feeling that I was laying the foundation of my work in Europe.

While my French journalism aspirations were taking off, my French lessons were going downhill fast. After Advanced 1 with Yves, Julie and I began to feel as though we had hit the wall. We had come to the stage where we had learnt all the grammar, although some aspects needed more practise than others. What we were doing in class was comprehension, written and oral. Which was what we needed, but it just wasn't working.

Even the handsomeness of Yves wasn't spurring us on. Sure he was good-looking in a French kind of way, but he just wasn't doing it for us. Perhaps it was the combination of his inability to speak English and our reluctance to speak French, but it wasn't long before we found him, well, dull.

Yves's class contained the worst combination of students for the level at which we were. Julie and I have soft voices and need time to prepare considered responses. Whenever the class was called upon to give a response we were never the first to answer—and even if we were, our voices would be drowned out by other, louder members of the class.

The key to avoiding humiliation in the classroom is this golden rule: always answer the questions that you know the answer to. That way, when there's a question that no-one can answer, the teacher won't ask you, they'll ask someone who hasn't contributed much. In our current class we couldn't even answer the questions we knew the answers to, such was the forcefulness of our classmates.

Comprehension was never our strong point, mainly because of a lack of confidence. In Yves's class our confidence was slowly diminishing. At the end of Advanced 1, Julie and I didn't feel ready to go up to the next level, but nor did we feel that repeating the class would help. We were stuck.

We talked about it and we realised that a time when our confidence grew was when it was just the two of us on the 'trip to Paris' with Yann, so we started toying with the idea of taking a term off and having private lessons.

One night after work we went to the Alliance to talk with someone about our options. We walked in, the Alliance was almost empty, and there sitting at the front desk was possibly the most beautiful man I have ever seen. He was a dead ringer for Jude Law—blond, tanned, slim build and the most piercing, shining blue eyes that twinkled when he spoke.

Looking back, he wasn't terribly helpful. Julie and I went through our options and for most of the time he just sat there smiling flirtingly with us. He only really spoke when we asked him a direct question like, 'What night of the week is the A1 class?'

We were still discussing what we should do when the *mec* suddenly got up and said, 'You will wait here'. He disappeared into the office, giving Julie and I a minute to quickly exchange 'Oh my God's!' before he returned with another *mec*, maybe his age. The other guy was a bit more feral and had a gap in his teeth, nowhere near as handsome as our blond friend. The reason he went and got this guy soon became clear. We assumed it was because he needed help understanding us, or he needed someone with a greater knowledge of classes. It was neither.

His friend did nothing and said nothing. He just stood in the doorway watching the proceedings. Yet, blond guy didn't seem to care. Of course he didn't. He had fetched his friend for the simple purpose of checking us out.

Eventually we decided that we would try to get Yann to give us some private lessons, so we asked the *mec* what was the cost of private tuition. 'Sixty-nine dollars with Yann', he said with a sly smile and a twinkle in his eye. Okay, it was cheesy, but Julie and I both went weak at the knees.

He told us that he would call Yann and then let us know and we left. It was amazing that we even got as far as the front gates before we just dissolved into squeals. In all our time at the Alliance, this was the first time we had ever come across a truly hot French guy. Naturally, Julie assured me that she was not going to pursue this hot young French guy. 'I feel like Laurant and I have a kind of relationship already', she told me seriously. 'I don't want to risk losing that.'

I did notice that, despite her intentions, Julie had flirted outrageously with the spunk. 'Best you don't mention that to Laurant!' I teased.

'I don't think he'd be interested,' she threw her head back defiantly, 'he's probably too busy on his *dates*'.

The next day I got a call at home. 'Hello, this is Douglas from the Alliance Française. You came in yesterday and you wanted private French lessons with Yann?'

'Yes', I replied. 'Are you the person who we spoke to?'

'Yes.' Hot damn, I thought, wait until Julie hears about this—I got a name!

Douglas told me that Yann was not available for private tuition but he had spoken to Yves who said he could do them. I wasn't too sure this was the solution because I really felt I had learnt very little during his classes, but Douglas's voice was so sexy and deep, I rapidly agreed and Julie and I signed up for private lessons with Yves.

Soon afterwards the Alliance Française put on a show as part of the Melbourne Arts Festival, dedicated to the works of Victor Hugo. It was held in a marquee out the front of the Victorian Arts Centre, which was done up in a style that looked like a cross between a carnival and a seventeenth century brothel—full of plush burgundy with gold fittings.

'You can pick up some home decorating hints!' Julie said to me. I laughed. Laughing at each other's homes had become a running joke. I often took the piss out of her Bachelor in Paris Pad ('When are Dean, Frank and Sammy dropping by?').

The night that Julie and I went to the marquee it was standing room only. We placed ourselves right in the centre of the back, next to the video equipment. We scanned the room for Douglas, hoping that he would be there. '*Où est Douglas?*' demanded Julie, impatiently.

The guy operating the video turned around. It was Douglas's mate, who we had affectionately named Toothless Thierry, except now he had had all his hair clippered off, to reveal quite a handsome face. Toothless Thierry was a funky guy. He wore checkered pants, a waistcoat and a street urchin cap—cool, but not drop-dead gorgeous like Douglas.

'*Ses cheveux sont disparus!*' whispered Julie. 'This guy is a real sleeper!' But he wasn't the guy we were there for. 'Where is Douglas?' we kept asking ourselves, looking around desperately, all the time Toothless Thierry was looking our way and smiling. He had a sweet smile and he was definitely beginning to grow on us.

Then we saw him. The show was a mixture of readings from the works of Victor Hugo, songs from *Les Misérables* and essays about his life and times, performed by the staff and students of the Alliance Française. And one of the staff was Douglas.

Douglas read out an essay critiquing the style of Victor Hugo. It was a subject that we were quite surprised he had the brains to know anything about, given his good looks and flirty personality. He had the audience hooked on every word with his sly smile and his occasional raised eyebrow and sparkling eyes. He looked cheeky and the audience loved it.

At the end of the performance, everyone came on stage and sang a version of 'Do You Hear The People Sing', and the players were introduced individually. Julie and I watched when it came to Douglas's turn; he raised a triumphant arm as the voiceover said, 'Benjamin!'

Our faces dropped. Benjamin? If hot guy was Benjamin, then who the hell was Douglas? Then it hit us. Toothless Thierry was Douglas. He was the only other person who was there when we went in to inquire about private tuition. And he had been standing next to us the whole time we were saying, 'Where is Douglas?'

We were at first horrified, but as the initial shock of our error passed, we realised it wasn't such a bad thing. Douglas hadn't looked at us with disgust; he had smiled and said hello. And we were just beginning to realise his potential.

Chapter 24
Christine, the woman Julie wants to be

Adjectives following the noun
une robe bleue
colour or shape
une fille française
nationality, origin, profession, religion
la porte ouverte
those formed by a past or present participal
une conversation complètement bête
those modified by an adverb

When we decided to skip a semester and have private lessons, we knew we were losing our class. They had all progressed and we were now a semester behind. We were actually kind of relieved. The class with Yves had been the only class we actually disliked. Sure, in other semesters there were students we found freakish and some even annoying, but we always considered them laughable. In Yves's class we just didn't like them.

As we suspected, our semester of private lessons with Yves didn't yield great results. We did exactly the same exercises we had done in the class-room situation—reading articles and discussing them—except now it was just Julie and me.

Our confidence, which was our last remaining obstacle in learning French, did not improve. In fact, it got worse. Being hounded by Yves individually sent our confidence plummeting. Still, we were optimistic. Maybe our next teacher would be Yann, or Aleksandra, and the fun would be put back into our lessons.

When we went to enrol, we asked who our teacher would be. The woman behind the counter told us that her name was Christine. 'Hmm, we haven't had her before', mused Julie.

'Who is your teacher normally?' asked Francoise.

'Yves', Julie replied.

'Well, Christine is his wife', she said. This bit of news surprised us. We knew that Yves was married to an Australian and all the teachers at the Alliance were supposed to be natives.

I had actually seen Christine before. One day Ky and I were having breakfast at a cafe opposite the South Melbourne Market and I saw Yves and his wife sitting outside. They were both reading the paper so it was impossible to see her face. All I could see was someone dressed in an old, baggy jumper who had really pale skin and red hair tied in a bun. Not someone who deserved a French husband, Julie had concluded when I described her.

The Christine we saw when we entered the classroom did not look a thing like the Christine I had seen at the market. She was wearing some very expensive corduroy pants in fisherman style and a baby blue, tracksuit material T-shirt with the sleeves and neck cut off. Her red hair was tied in loose knots on her head and her make-up was impeccable. She was tall and slim and a true bohemian.

'Welcome!' she said with a huge smile. She asked us our names and whether we had studied at the Alliance before (pretty standard questions) and then asked who our teacher was. When we said Yves, she grabbed her heart dramatically and laughed and said, 'The love of my life!'

Christine was clearly French but she also spoke so clearly we had absolutely no trouble understanding her. She was always so enthusiastic when someone got something right that it made us want to answer questions. And she never called on anyone in class, so the students were never in fear.

Simply, Christine was so cool we didn't just want to be around her, we wanted to be her. In the car on the way home, we couldn't stop talking about how beautiful and how cool Christine was. We decided without question she was certainly worthy of being married to a French man.

As we pulled up in the car the next week we noticed there were an extraordinary amount of cars and people in Robe Street, and after driving up and down several times we ended up parking in the next street. There was obviously something happening at the Alliance, because the parking spaces out the front were sealed off with witches' hats and there seemed to be a lot of people using walkie-talkies and wandering around the grounds.

We were a little nervous. The world was waiting for the US to invade Iraq and France was one of the few Western nations to support the Arabs and condemn the activities of the US. Walking through the gates we were stopped by a security guard. 'Are you two students here?' she asked.

'Yes, we have a six o'clock class with Christine', I said, showing her my books.

She waved us in. We walked into class and were taking our seats when we could see people start walking into the building. 'There are a lot of very well-dressed people walking into the Alliance tonight, no?' said Christine. 'It's because the ambassador is here.'

She said these words in English and to our surprise we realised Christine spoke with a very strong Australian accent. Over the next few weeks we learnt more about Christine. The first surprise was that she was really an Australian. We couldn't believe it when, during lessons, she used English to explain particularly complicated points. She spoke English with a very strong Australian accent and French with a strong French accent, which was so reassuring to Julie and me because at the time we were still speaking French with an appalling Australian accent.

Christine lived for some time in Paris where she studied at the Sorbonne, which explained why her French was so good. During the day she worked as a translator and both she and Yves worked at the Alliance at night. She was a real Francophile—she loved French film and culture, and she was obsessed with fashion.

Gradually, with Christine's help, our confidence resurfaced and we started to actually enjoy going to class again. Mainly we wanted to see what Christine was wearing. No matter how dressed up or down she was, she always looked immaculate and groovy.

We wanted to be just like Christine, and in Julie's mind she was on the right track. The love letters between Julie and Laurant were continuing, and soon she would meet him for what we were calling The Weekend d'Amour. In Julie's grand plan, she would persuade Laurant to move out here, just like Yves had done, and we could all hang out together being funky Francophiles.

The people in our new class were still freaks—but unlike the freaks in the previous class, these weren't nasty freaks, they were more like the freaks we encountered all the way through Beginners and Intermediate. There were a couple of middle-aged women, who weren't very good (yay!) and a few guys who looked to be in their thirties and were about as good as us. Like us, everyone had a good time and adored Christine, so there wasn't any of the politics and bitchiness we had been experiencing in Yve's class.

Pierre's name was Peter and he hated being called Pierre. Yet, he explained to us, all the teachers he had had insisted on calling him Pierre. The reason he hated the name was he thought that it gave the impression that he was either French or considered himself to be French, which then laden him with the pressure of having to be really good at French. He wasn't bad, but he wasn't great either. Like Chris, what he did have was a desire to answer every question, regardless of whether he knew the answer, or whether someone else should really be given a chance to have a go.

Meanwhile, Douglas always smiled and greeted us on the way to class. Benjamin was sometimes there and he always stared and smiled a smile that made us go weak at the knees, but never said anything to us, unless we asked him a question.

One night after class, Julie and I were standing at the counter looking at the flyers advertising up-coming events. The Alliance was extremely busy and students were clambering to reach the front desk. I was talking small talk to Benjamin when there was a tap on my shoulder.

'Excuse me.' I turned around to see a young woman standing behind me. 'I'm sorry to interrupt, but can I please just say goodbye to Benjamin?'

Thinking she must have been a friend of his, I let her push in next to me. She smiled, tilted her head and crooned, *'Bon soir, Benjamin ...'*

'Bon soir!' replied Benjamin. And with that, the woman turned and left. Benjamin turned and continued the conversation with me as though that kind of interruption was perfectly normal. And it probably was.

More than any classes we had ever done, Christine's were fun. Some things we did in every class. We always had to bring an article from a French newspaper and discuss it with the class and we always watched a news item on the TV and answered questions about it. But there were other things that were equally fun.

We listened to music and had to fill in the gaps in the lyrics sheet, and we had grammar auctions, where Christine would write sentences on the board that may or may not be grammatically correct, and we had to bid on them. If the sentence were correct you'd get the points, if not you didn't—unless you could correct it.

We also had to read articles and discuss them with the class, just as we did with Yves. One night we had our heads down reading an article, when I heard a thwack on the window. I looked up and there was a magazine with Patrick Bruel on the cover pressed right up against the window. I didn't know what to do. It was obviously intended for me, but I didn't want to laugh or disrupt the class, because I didn't want to have to explain it.

'Oh my God!' suddenly Julie was laughing hysterically. Christine and the class looked up and the magazine disappeared.

We knew it was Yann, but when we walked out of class we couldn't see him. Walking through the front yard, though, we heard a deep, sleazy voice, 'Bonjour.' We turned around and saw Yann standing under a tree. Well, it looked like Yann, and it clearly was Yann, but it was Yann's body inhabited by a porn star.

He was smoking and nodding slowly, trying to be very cool and whenever we asked him a question like, 'How are you?' or 'How's work?' he replied in a slow, deep voice, 'Good. It's all good'. If he was trying to appear sexy to us it was to his own detriment. After asking a few questions and all being answered with 'good', we ran out of things to talk about and went home.

Julie and I became so inspired that we started watching the French news in the mornings, borrowing books from the library and listening to music. We also resolved to participate in more Alliance activities. We had had a good time at the Victor Hugo night and we really were keen to practise and perfect our French as much as possible. So we booked in for a day trip planned by the Alliance Française.

The excursion was to francophone wineries in the Yarra Valley region and was to be conducted entirely in French. We were told we would be taken on a tour around the wineries, have a lunch, and listen to a talk by the *Age* wine writer about the history of francophone wineries in Victoria.

When we first tried to make a booking, Douglas told us that it was fully booked, but he took our numbers and said he'd call if something came up. He called a couple of days later and said that because demand had been so big they had decided to put on another bus.

I was becoming very fond of Douglas. He was gorgeous in every way. A couple of times I bumped into him in St Kilda and he always had the time to stop for a chat. There was nothing sleazy about him though, he was just a really nice guy. Every week when we walked into the Alliance, his face would light up. I hoped he would be coming on the wine trip, and there was a good chance that he would—he attended most Alliance functions.

Whilst Julie appreciated that Douglas was a nice guy and despite my encouragement, he didn't set her world on fire. 'He's just not hot', she told me.

'He is hot', I replied.

'Not in an Olivier Martinez way', she said.

'You said he was hot.'

'I did not! I said he was funky. I think of Douglas like a…' she grappled for the words, 'like a French brother. A *frère*'.

I remembered a time when a guy would just have to be French for him to be hot in the eyes of Julie. What was she now, *picky?* I wondered if her proxy love interest, Laurant, was responsible.

On the day of the excursion we arrived at the Alliance early in the morning. At first we were disappointed because most people were over forty and there was not one teacher or student who we knew. The only person who was familiar to us was Jean-Philippe, the director. Out the front there was a coach and a smaller mini bus.

After rollcall Julie and I got onto the coach. There were two seats left but they weren't together, so we asked the woman, who was by herself, if she would mind moving next to the man behind her. She completely freaked out—apparently she had chosen that seat specifically because it was by the window—but when we assured her that she could have the window seat next to the man, she reluctantly agreed. It was a reminder of the age difference between our travelling companions and us.

The Yarra Valley is only just over an hour out of Melbourne, but in that hour, something odd happened. Ever since we had started going to the Alliance, Jean-Philippe had been the director. He looked as though he was in his forties and looked traditionally French—on the skinny side with clippered hair, and always wearing corduroys and a roll neck skivvy. We had never even considered him as a potential—until now. There was something about the way he had control of the microphone at the front of the bus that gave him a certain power and presence. He joked with the passengers in a very French way, but he also had an underlying depth and seriousness.

We got off the bus at the Daniel Portet winery, which was a beautiful Tuscan-style building—dusty orange walls, French windows and rosemary bushes surrounding it. Daniel Portet was something else; one of those guys that just seems to get sexier with age. He was tanned and grey-haired and well dressed and had an arrogant French attitude. He took us on a tour of the winemaking facilities, which was interesting.

Afterwards we had a buffet lunch on long trestle tables, of tomato and cheese salads, quiches, bread and sausage meat and wines. We sat with an expat French woman who was a lot like Aleksandra. She was really into cinema and encouraging us to speak French, something we were still uncomfortable doing.

Meanwhile, Julie was trying to make meaningful eye contact with Jean-Philippe. ('I'm not *interested* in him. I'm just *toying* with him.') He wasn't taking the bait and hardly even acknowledged us.

During the lunch, we listened to the talk by the *Age* wine writer. It was pretty interesting. Apparently Daniel Portet's father runs a sister winery in France, where Daniel learnt his profession. Aside from a mad rush to coffee, which sent some of the staff into a frenzy, it was a very relaxing lunch.

Afterwards, Julie and I bought some wine and then wandered around the grounds. Spending the day with a bunch of older people wasn't that bad. A funny moment happened in the yard, when a large English woman rushed up to us and said with urgency, 'Did I hear cake? Can it be true?' When we said yes, she rushed off like the rabbit in *Alice In Wonderland*. Then we all boarded the bus to go to the next winery, Yerling. Everyone was jostling to get a place on the big bus, apparently the minibus wasn't exactly comfortable, and some of the shoving wasn't nice.

Yerling wasn't as romantic as Portet—it's a modern building and the people who took the wine tastings looked like high school students who were reciting things they had been told. But we had a glass of wine and walked around the gourmet food shop and I bought a couple of things.

We thought we would get back to the bus early—we were envisaging a similar rush like before—and were horrified at the number of people who had 'reserved' their seats by placing personal items on them. We were tired by the end of the day so it was a very quiet trip home.

When we arrived at the Alliance, who should happen to be walking past but Douglas with a little puppy. It was almost too small for a lead, so eventually Douglas picked him up. As everyone got off the bus, those who knew Douglas rushed up to him to coo at his puppy—but he kept one eye on the puppy and the other on Julie.

It's a funny thing that happens when a group of total strangers go on a trip to the country—it's like some sort of strange bond is formed. As we all said goodbye there was a lot of kissing, hugging and promises to stay in touch (except for Julie and I who really didn't talk to anyone except each other). As we were driving out of the car park, Jean-Philippe gave us a wave, which was bizarre seeing as next time we saw him he didn't even acknowledge our presence. It was obvious that Douglas was attracted to Julie but she ignored all the signs. She had other things on her mind—she was leaving for France and The Weekend *d'Amour*.

Chapter 25
Margie conducts her first interview entirely in French

Expressions of comparison

Plus...que (More than)

Ce bijou est plus cher que tu voudras.

That jewel is more expensive than you want.

Moins...que (Less than)

Cette région est moins pittoresque que l'autre.

That region is less picturesque than the other.

The French Film Festival was scheduled directly after Julie's return from Europe. Every year there is one film that opens the festival and is promoted on all the posters and press releases. It's generally the most commercial, or the one deemed to be more palatable for an audience who may not be familiar with French films.

This year it was *Sur Mes Lèvres* (Read My Lips). It starred Vincent Cassel, who is a huge name in French cinema. Cassel began his career in the French version of *Single White Female,* which was called *L'Appartement.* He was labelled a heart-throb because of his cute good looks, but in recent times had been involved in some less mainstream French films, as well as a couple of Hollywood flicks. He played one of the dodgy Russians in the Nicole Kidman film *Birthday Girl.*

Co-starring beside Cassel was Emmanuelle Devos, a well-known actress in France and one with a solid body of work behind her. Devos played Carla, a deaf secretary, pushed around and taken advantage of by the men in her office, who considered her of little consequence if they considered her at all. When she is given permission to hire an assistant, she decides to hire Cassel, a rough ex-con whom she hopes will teach her to be a little bit bad.

Anne-Marie from Palace Films called me and asked me if I wanted to do an interview with Emmanuelle Devos, and of course I said yes. It would look good for further work I wanted to do for French magazines, plus it would be good experience to build on my interviews with other French actors.

This year the festival was held at the old George cinema in Fitzroy Street, St Kilda. I went there for the screening of *Read My Lips* and saw a few people from the Alliance, including Jean-Philippe and Douglas.

The big difference between interviewing Devos and Jaoui was, while Jaoui spoke some English (her English was probably as good as my French at that stage), Devos spoke not one word of English.

Even Julie, who refused to believe we were anything other than Real French *Filles*, was shocked when I told her. 'Oh no!' she said, alarm showing on her face. Then, after a couple of seconds' thought, she regained her composure. 'It will be fine, Margie. Just ask her to speak slowly. And if there are any words you don't understand, just call me on my *portable* and I'll get Laurant to translate.' The interview coincided with her Weekend *d'Amour*.

While preparing for the interview I began to get a little panicked, even though I figured I had it all worked out. I could write the questions in advance so there would be no problem there. And if I asked her to speak very clearly, it wouldn't matter if I didn't understand everything she said at the time, I could translate it later.

Had the opportunity presented itself a few months earlier, while we were in Yves's class, I doubt I would have accepted it. But Christine's classes had lifted our confidence to the point where I really believed it was possible to conduct an interview entirely in French.

There would only be a couple of possible hiccups. One, if Devos couldn't understand my accent or if she lost her temper at my bad accent. But more immediately, there are words that are very particular to cinema—words like filming, director, stars—which are not words we had ever studied. I looked through all my textbooks and thankfully there was an everyday usage one that had a chapter on movies and going to the cinema, and all the translations I needed were there.

The interview was scheduled for seven o'clock in the morning and I was up at six, chain-smoking and going over my notes. Right on time the international operator called and connected me to Devos, and I launched into my speech.

'*Bonjour, je m'appelle Margaret Ambrose. Je suis une journaliste et je travaille au gURLpool. Mon français est un peu mauvais. Alors, il faut que vous parliez très clairement et très doucement, s'il vous plaît …*'

Well, she didn't laugh.

And she understood what I said.

So I launched into the first question. 'The Carla at the end of the film is very different from the Carla we see at the beginning …'

'Yes, she is assertive and stronger. At the start she is so timid and insignificant. Paul transforms her. By the end she is in love, and the change that love makes to her character is incredible.'

Excellent! She was speaking clearly and, more importantly, I was understanding every word she said. 'Yes, but transformed into what? Certainly not a particularly nice person?' I continued.

'No, Carla is a person who wants to take revenge. She becomes a monster! Jacques Audiard [the director] said to me, just because some-one has gone through bad times, it doesn't mean that when she has power she will be kind to other people. This is true, but the audience does like Carla. I think that people can relate to her. When I read it, I found *Read My Lips* was a magnificent story. It is very rare to find a role like Carla—very interesting.'

'Is it an insult to tell you that you play her very well?' I laughed.

'No, I was very similar to Carla when I was a teenager. Sometimes I was very shy and timid. I went back to my teenage years. It was very important to understand these feelings and to be able to bring them to the role of Carla.'

'The character of Paul is also transformed …'

'Absolutely. What one of them is missing, the other provides. At the beginning Paul is a person who thinks only of himself. He is a loner. Love changes him, too.'

'The film can be quite violent and, of course, there are a lot of scenes set on a rooftop. Was filming gruelling?' I asked. At this point my luck momentarily faltered. Devos began to get excited and animated and of course her speech sped up. I knew she was talking about Cassel, but between the laughter and the speed, I hardly understood a word. But afterwards, and after a lot of rewinding, playing and more rewinding, I was able to get most of it.

'Not at all. It was really enjoyable. Jacques Audiard was enormously supportive and Vincent Cassel is hilarious. It was relaxed and a bit of fun. When we were on the roof we had to wear safety harnesses, which was an unusual experience.'

'Over the past few years there have been several French films that have done well in Australia, such as *Le Placard* and *Amélie*', I said, changing tack.

'Well. *Amélie* was a very pretty film, but you know, that is not the real Paris ... I think Australians appreciate film. In France, we don't know if a film is really Australian or British or American, but I know there are many good actors who are Australian and I liked *Moulin Rouge* very much.'

'*Moulin Rouge* wasn't the real Paris either ...' I interrupted.

'No, but it was a great story. That is what is the most important thing for me, whether I am in the film or going to the cinema. And *Read My Lips* is an incredible story.'

The perfect end to the interview, I thought, so I thanked her, said goodbye and hung up. Going back to bed sounded good, but sleep was impossible. I was so revved up. All I could think was that I had just done an interview entirely in French and I was filled with a feeling that I could do anything.

As I lay in bed, heart pounding and unable to sleep, the phone rang. Thinking it must be Palace Films, I answered in a professional voice, 'Margaret speaking'.

I could hear sobbing on the other end of the line, but no-one spoke. I sat up. 'Hello?'

'It's me', whimpered Julie.

'Julie, are you okay?' I asked. Julie was in France and this was supposed to be The Weekend *d'Amour*.

'Sorry to call in the middle of the night', she said.

'That's okay, what's happened? Did Laurant do something? Is he a bastard?'

At that, Julie burst into tears. 'It was horrible!' she said. 'He's retarded.'

'Jules, he couldn't be that bad', I said, trying to calm her down. 'What did he do?'

'No!' she shouted angrily. 'He really is retarded! He's got Downs syndrome. He is retarded and he *looks* retarded!'

I was gobsmacked. Julie explained that the whole Trignant family—Madame Trignant, Monsieur Trignant and their retarded son, Laurant, had met her at the airport. 'Well, I did learn something,' Julie whined, 'people with Downs syndrome look the same in every country'.

It didn't make sense. 'How could he work for Concorde?' I asked.

'It's a program they have for handicapped people. Margie, Laurant is severely disabled. He can't even dress himself. And he can't speak English—he doesn't even know there is another language other than French. And he speaks so quickly, I can't even understand him.'

'But he wrote you all those beautiful letters in English!'

'His mother wrote them for him. And they weren't love letters, they were just friendly letters.' Julie had been given Laurant's room to sleep in and Laurant slept on the fold-out bed in the study. 'He didn't mind', she explained, somewhat bitterly. 'He thought it was an adventure.'

The first night there, Julie explained, she was so shattered she got photos of her family and friends and put them on the bedside table for comfort. The next day Madame Trignant took Julie to show her the town and do some shopping. When they returned home, Julie went to her room to rest 'I was on the bed looking at the photos when I noticed there was an extra picture among them', she said. 'Laurant had been in my room. He put a picture of himself with the photos of my friends!'

'Oh. My. God.' It was all I could say.

'He wants to be my friend!'

Suddenly I had a thought. 'But what about all those dates? Who was he going out with, retarded girls?'

'How the hell should I know?' Julie replied sharply.

Despite her hysterical call to me, Julie assured me that she had shown no signs of shock to the family, who were actually very sweet and hospitable.

There was nothing I could say that would take away the pain of disappointment for Julie. All I could do was assure her that there were plenty more *poisson* (fish) in the *mer* (sea), which at least made her laugh.

Later that day, Julie called me from the airport. She had checked in and was waiting to board her flight. 'How did the rest of the visit go?' I asked. Julie sounded chirpier than she had in the last call.

'Oh it was fine', she chuckled. 'But I have to tell you something that is funny.'

Julie was catching a late flight, so she had dinner with the family and then went to her room to pack. When she came out, she noticed that Laurant was dressed in a suit and tie and had his hair combed neatly. In his hands were a bunch of flowers. 'Where are you going?' asked Julie.

Laurant reeled off an explanation rapidly in French so Julie didn't understand a word. But it was Sunday night, so she suspected that he was going on his date.

Madame Trignant explained to Julie that every two weeks Laurant goes on a date. Monsieur Trignant added with a wicked chuckle that he takes his son to 'How you say ... a brothel'.

I gasped.

'Margie', Julie laughed at my horror, 'they are a very respectable, decent family. Laurant is twenty-nine—he has sexual urges, but he doesn't have the capacity to deal with them responsibly. They take him to a brothel and he gets it out of his system'.

I was too shocked to speak. Julie laughed. 'And you're okay with this?' I asked.

'Well, this way at least he won't be attacking women on the street!' Julie added. 'And he does take flowers, which is nice.'

'And Margie', she sighed, 'what the hell can I do?'

When Lincoln came home from cricket I gave him an extra long hug. 'Please, please, please tell me I will never have to date again?'

'You won't ever have to date again babe', he said, cracking open a can of beer and turning on the TV. Okay, he's about as far removed from a French man as possible, I thought, but I seriously didn't care.

Chapter 26

Julie's illusions
of Paris are shattered

Causes

Positive: Grâce à (thanks to)
Elle a trouvé un appartement grâce à ses amies.
She found an apartment thanks to her friends.

Negative: à cause de (because of)
Le match a été annulé à cause du mauvais temps.
The game was cancelled because of the bad weather.

Neutral: en raison de (because of)
Le magasin sera fermé en raison des fêtes de Pâques.
The shop will be closed because of the Easter holidays.

Laurant was never spoken of again. When Julie returned she seemed happy and relaxed, and high on her dose of French culture. When people asked her about her trip she spoke of the restaurants she went to, the clothes she bought and the charming family she stayed with. The Laurant debacle hadn't dulled her enthusiasm for all things French—in fact, her visit to the country had fuelled it.

As always, Julie and I mapped out our French Film Festival plan of action. It worked out well this year, because there were no films during the week. Instead, we had two weekends of movies.

'He's killed someone and been to prison for it', said Julie seriously, as we drove to the festival.

'What?' I asked. 'How do you know that?'

'I asked my stepdad. He knows all about this kind of stuff. In Europe you can always tell when someone has killed someone else because they tattoo themselves with those symbols in prison. They wear it like a badge of honour.'

'But those symbols could mean anything.'

'No,' said Julie, matter-of-factly, 'I described them exactly, and my stepfather had no doubts'.

It took a minute for this information to sink in. Jean-Philippe, the director of the Alliance Française, a murderer? 'No', I refused to believe it. 'How could an ex-con be director of the Alliance? He has meetings with the ambassador for God's sake!'

'Well', answered Julie, 'Australia is a long way from France ... an ideal place to send someone you want to get rid of. Who knows? He might have been owed a favour. Or, his father could be someone important'.

I sat there in silence. Eventually Julie shrugged and said, 'Okay, so I didn't ask my stepdad and he didn't tell me that those tattoos belong to murderers. But, if you ask me, that's the only plausible solution'.

Honestly, Julie had the worst imagination.

We started off the festival with *Astérix et Obélix*, which starred Gerard Depardieu as Obelix. It was hilarious and very commercial. The next day we saw *Monsieur Batignole*, which was an amazing true story of a family who started out as collaborators but who turned out saving some children. It's a part of the war history that is seldom mentioned. France has always been racist, especially anti-Semitic, and during the Second World War a lot of people in Paris not only went along with the Nazis, but worked with them to implement their right-wing politics.

It was really an incredible story and it wasn't surprising that it was picked up in the following months and released in cinemas nationally. To our disappointment, though, that weekend we saw no-one we knew from the Alliance, so while we loved the movies, the experience wasn't all that special. The next weekend was different, with high highs and very low lows.

Irréversible caused a sensation when it was released in France, and there was a lot of opposition to it being shown at the French Film Festival in

Australia, because it was said to be incredibly violent. Julie and I agreed that we didn't have a problem with violence, and plus we were curious as to what all the fuss was about.

But the clincher was that the star of *Irréversible* was Vincent Cassel. His co-star was French actress Monica Bellucci, who was a massive star in France as well as being well-known elsewhere in the world for her role in the *Matrix* movies.

There was only going to be one showing of *Irréversible,* so Julie rang and booked a week in advance. And it was a good thing too, because she was told it was practically sold out. Julie and I quite rightly felt like we could cope with extreme violence. We see it all the time in Hollywood blockbusters—even in art house movies—and when confronted with the most appalling violence we were able to reconcile it by the fact that it was, after all, just a film.

Irréversible started in a burst of violence. Vincent Cassel was running through the dark halls of a gay bar, passing couples in various sex acts, out of his mind with anger, looking for someone called Tenir. The search went on for ages, and for much of the time the screen was black, except for bursts of lights. It was often hard to work out what was going on.

Eventually he found this man Tenir and a fight followed. Vincent Cassel was lying on the floor having his head smashed in with a fire extinguisher. There was blood and body parts everywhere, but it was the sound that was excruciating. Practically everyone in the cinema was looking away from the screen and covering their ears with their hands.

The scene then moved on to a taxi, where Cassel and a friend were desperately looking for the gay club Rectum. Aside from being highly agitated, Cassel looked in perfect health. This movie was obviously going back in time. There were the same flashes of light and jerking camera movements and still the yelling and screaming. It was very uncomfortable to watch.

The next scene was just as bad. Cassel and his friend were harassing a prostitute for information. The next scene showed the pair standing on the street, emergency vehicles in the background, looking shocked. Two men approach them and tell them that for a price they will take them to a hooker who knows who committed the crime.

Then there was a much happier Cassel and friend standing outside a house where there is a party, laughing, when they notice a commotion. They stop someone and ask what's going on and they are told that someone has been raped. They walked forward to have a look and Cassel's face drops. There's Bellucci on a stretcher covered in blood. 'Ma femme', he screams. 'Ma femme!'

So we know what's going to happen next.

The character played by Monica Bellucci is trying to cross the road but there is too much traffic, so a hooker suggests she take the under-pass instead. So she walks down into the tunnel. It's a real-time scene so it seems to take forever. Halfway through the tunnel she sees a pimp arguing with a hooker. As she walks past, the pimp steps back and bumps into her. He turns around and the hooker runs off. He pulls out a knife.

The scene lasted ten minutes. I don't even know how to describe it, except to say that it was explicit and violent. And unfortunately, we were having a good comprehension night, so we were able to understand most of what he was saying as he was raping her. 'You think because you are so beautiful, you can have anything you want?'

At the end of the rape the criminal kicks her in the face. That's when Julie and I left. I noticed a steady stream of people leaving the cinema throughout the rape scene, and even before that, but I was staggered to see that the once sold-out cinema was now half-empty.

A lot of people were standing and sitting in the foyer, looking quite shattered. A representative from Palace was walking around trying to calm people down. I couldn't say a word, partly because I didn't know what to say and partly because I felt that if I tried to express what I was feeling I would lose it completely.

Julie was the opposite. She was furious and she wanted everyone to know about it. She wanted to know how a movie like this was allowed to be shown. 'Why do I have to see that?' she demanded angrily. 'How the fuck did that get past the censors?'

Part Three: Advanced

I'd never seen her so angry. She wasn't just furious at the censors. 'What was Vincent Cassel thinking? Why did he do it?' She was pleading for answers, and was frustrated that there were none.

I still hadn't said anything. I was just trying to hold it together. Every time someone brushed past me I felt like screaming. I just wanted to leave. Our car was parked in the car park which, although well lit, added to our terror. It took Julie forever to find her keys because her hands were shaking. By the time we got in the car we were a mess and Julie was concerned about her ability to drive.

We were so shattered we couldn't bear to be apart, and we needed a drink badly, so we went to The Lounge in Elwood. We got as far as the door when we decided that it was a really bad idea. It was full of people drinking and laughing and flirting with each other. Not only would we have people touching us, we'd have them hitting on us. Besides, neither Julie nor I were convinced that at some stage we wouldn't start crying.

Even though my place was a mess, I knew it was empty and it was close so I suggested we go back there. It felt great to be back home. I made a coffee and we talked some more about the movie. Of course there is a very good reason why movies like *Irréversible* are made. The violence we get in movies is so sanitised that we get an unrealistic idea of it. The rape scene in *Irréversible* is in real time and shows what rape is like—the terror and the length of time the terror lasts—and it doesn't skip or gloss over bits.

Julie and I could rationalise this, but we were still disturbed. Over the next few months certain parts haunted me: the sound of the rapists' voice, the blood on her face, what she was wearing. I wanted more than anything to forget it, but it kept coming back.

After a couple of coffees we were no longer frightened, we were left feeling sickened and repulsed. Everything about that movie made us ill. Unfortunately, it was set in Paris. And this was freaking Julie out the most. She had spent her life dreaming of this city, and now when she thought about it all she saw was a filthy tunnel, pain and humiliation. She was so upset.

'Well, we don't know for sure that it was in Paris', I suggested.

Immediately her expression changed. 'That's right', she said. 'It could have been any city.'

'I'm sure it was Marseille', I continued.

'Do you think so? Do you really think so?' Julie was almost pleading.

'Yeah', I said, totally unconvinced, 'I'm sure it was Marseille'.

I put on some French CDs but it didn't seem to be changing her mood. Then I put on *Entre Deux,* the Patrick Bruel CD full of old, romantic French songs. It was exactly what she needed.

Julie sat in the kitchen with the CD cover, singing along to all the songs. Of course, all the songs of this period are cheery and innocent—romanticising the times. They heralded a time when everything was sweet and Julie couldn't get enough of it. After about an hour, and a few cups of coffee, she seemed less angry and was able to leave.

I wasn't frightened in the way that one becomes scared after seeing a horror movie; I wasn't jumping at every little noise. I was depressed. And with good reason. What *Irréversible* had shown was what could happen to anyone at anytime. There was nothing reckless about the Bellucci character; she was just crossing the road. Sure, in hindsight, she probably should have become concerned when she saw the pimp arguing with the hooker, but how many of us have sensed danger and just continued, telling ourselves we're being silly?

The fact is, I turned over in my head, that women are totally at the mercy of men. The only thing that stops every woman being raped is that there are men who think it's wrong. Women's safety is totally dependent on the morals of men. We have no power. These thoughts were thick in my head.

The only way a woman can protect herself properly is by being armed, I concluded. That is the only way a woman can control her own safety. So that night I resolved to get a gun. I didn't feel safe and I knew that the only way I would feel safe is if I could protect myself.

Julie wasn't convinced. 'How would a gun have helped that woman?' she asked. 'At what point could she have pulled it out? He had a knife at her throat before she realised what was happening.'

Part Three: Advanced

Ky was reluctant to tell me what to do or to even imply that an idea of mine was silly but she was concerned. 'I think you should wait until you are calmer and then make a decision', she suggested.

'What, do you want me to get raped?' I yelled. 'Because that's what will happen if I don't have a gun! I will never be safe and I will never feel safe—is that what you want?'

I had never experienced a sense of such vulnerability. How could I live like this? It continued the next day. In the middle of the night I had woken suddenly to the sound of a fire extinguisher crushing Vincent Cassel's head. In the morning I was exhausted. I felt totally exposed and in danger.

We had another two films scheduled for that afternoon and we were desperately hoping that they would restore our faith in everything French, which was currently in tatters. There was a two-hour break between films so we brought along our homework to do at the bar between sessions.

The first film was called *Grégoire Moulin Versus Humanity,* and it was a light-weight, pretty lame comedy. In one scene the protagonist was left tied to a kitchen cupboard, on his stomach in the middle of a gay party. I saw Julie squirm uncomfortably and I felt sick. Yet the whole cinema was laughing. What's wrong with all these people, I thought, how can they think this is funny? Instead of making me feel better, I felt more isolated in my fear.

Judging by the look on people's faces as they left the movie, they had thought it was pretty good. Julie and I couldn't get excited about it. Well, that's it, I thought. *Irréversible* has robbed us of the ability to enjoy French films. But it could have just been a crap movie, I thought. I was still hopeful.

We went to The Lobby, the bar next to the cinema, which was pretty groovy and had lots of couches and tables and booths, and ordered a drink. We were doing revision on pronouns, which we had nailed, so the exercises should have taken us a matter of minutes. But because we stopped after every question to chat and gossip, it took a lot longer.

Or I should say to hypothesise. Julie had a theory on everything, not just Jean-Philippe and his murderous past. She had Christine and Yves's courtship all figured out. She had figured out what Benjamin and Douglas would be like as lovers, and what Yann would be like as a father.

After about half an hour another movie finished and people started to pour into the bar, including a lot of people from the Alliance. Christine and Yves stopped by to say hello to some people and on the way out Christine noticed us and stopped to chat, but Yves, who stayed in the background, told her they had to go.

That wasn't unusual. Whenever we saw Yves, he scuttled off somewhere. And Julie had a theory about that, too. 'Remember that night we were talking to Yves?' she asked. 'Yves was sitting at a table with Christine and I went up and told him we were here? Well Christine said to him, "Is that your class?" '

She looked triumphant, but I had apparently missed the point. She sighed 'Obviously, Christine has said something about us, his beautiful young students and now Yves doesn't want to speak to us because he is worried that he will get his ass kicked by Christine.'

Obviously.

Soon we saw Douglas and Jean-Philippe doing the schmoozing thing with a group of older people. When Douglas saw us, his face lit up and he held up a bottle of champagne as if to offer some. I smiled and nodded and he came over with the champagne and two glasses.

Although we always smiled and said hello to each other, the fact was that Douglas had never had a long, decent conversation with either Julie or myself. We hadn't even officially introduced ourselves. In fact, the only reason we believed his name to be Douglas was because Benjamin was Benjamin.

I had not so secretly harboured hopes for Julie and Douglas. In my mind they were perfectly suited to each other; they were both young, funky dressers, sweet and loved animals. And he was French. This could be the great romance for her. Yet Julie had never taken the bait.

She had agreed with me on all these points, but she was still having trouble getting past the missing tooth. Nothing that can't be fixed with a bit of dental work, I assured her. She did admit that he certainly looked a lot better with his short hair. Still, Benjamin best fit the mould of her ideal French man—in appearance at least. In my opinion, Benjamin was too flamboyant and frivolous.

As Douglas approached with the champagne, I hoped that Julie wouldn't notice the socks and sandals ensemble he had happening on his feet. She didn't seem to, plus he stood with the gappy side of his smile facing me and not her.

I needn't have worried. As Douglas walked towards us, Julie suddenly sat up straight, pulled her off-the-shoulder top further off the shoulder, lowered her head, and smiled seductively at him. Well, this is interesting, I thought.

Douglas poured us some champagne and started talking about the film festival. In particular he liked a film called *To Have and To Be,* and another, which was a documentary about deaf children.

'I thought it was really, really good.' He smiled. 'I was very interested in it because I know how to do sign language. I have a lot of deaf friends.'

'Oh', I replied. 'How do you come to have a lot of deaf friends?' I thought it was a reasonable question, but for a moment Douglas looked at me as though he didn't know how to respond to such an odd demand.

'I don't know,' he shrugged, 'when I worked in a bar I had one friend who was deaf'.

Okay, well it didn't really answer my question—I suspect something vital was lost in the translation—but on the upside Julie had to be impressed by his generosity to the disabled.

'We saw *Irréversible* last night', Julie told him.

'Ooh,' said Douglas, 'that film has had a lot of publicity. It is very violent apparently'.

'It was awful', said Julie. 'We left halfway through because we couldn't watch it any more.'

Douglas shook his head. 'I have not seen it and I don't want to see it. You know, I just do not like violent movies like that.'

Douglas had to go off and serve champagne to other people. Clearly Julie was smitten. 'Didn't I tell you?' I said triumphantly. 'Lots of deaf friends, hates violent movies. He's a really nice guy, Jules.' Judging by the slight blush on her face, Julie agreed.

'Aaah!' We heard an exclamation behind us and turned around. There was Aleksandra, our teacher for Beginners and most of Intermediate, who we hadn't seen for over a year. Aleksandra may have aged a year but she was still as sexy as ever, in a leopard skin top and kerchief around her neck.

Aleksandra was so pleased to see us and so happy that we had continued to study French. *'Nous sommes avancées maintenant'*, said Julie proudly. Aleksandra went into hysterics when she saw that we were sitting in a bar doing our homework. 'I remember all the *prendre un pots!*' she said.

She couldn't stay chatting for long because she was going into a movie, but she was clearly thrilled to have seen us. With all of this socialising, we weren't getting a whole lot of work done and so we decided to put our heads down and do some work. Just as it always is when you think you've got something nailed, we soon came to a question that had us stumped. No matter which way we looked at the question, we didn't know the answer. 'Hey', I suggested, 'you could go up and ask Douglas'.

Julie jumped at that suggestion and next time she caught his eye she beckoned him over, flirtatiously. Douglas looked thoughtfully at the question for a few moments and then said, 'I think it is this one, but I'm not very good with French grammar because I am from Belgium'.

Julie's face fell.

When he walked off, Julie looked at me with despair. I sprang into damage control. 'Think about the funkiness; think about his puppy; think about his hatred of violent films ...'

Julie said nothing. Despite this unexpected turn of events, we had had a good afternoon socialising and also getting our homework done. *Irréversible* was still haunting us, but we felt a little more relaxed. The drive home changed that. We were driving down Carlisle Street and stopped at the lights to make a right-hand turn into Barkly Street. Pedestrians crossed in front of the car except for an old bum, who stood in the middle of the road and suddenly started yelling. Julie and I were already on heightened terror alert and immediately snapped our locks shut.

'You fucking show pony!' the man yelled at a woman standing at the lights across the street. 'You think you're so fucking hot, well you're not. You fucking bitch, fuck me.'

'Oh my God, oh my God!' whined Julie. I felt like someone had me by the throat and couldn't utter a word. We were stuck in the middle of the intersection with no escape.

The old derro didn't even know this woman—she was just a tourist with a backpack—and we didn't know what had transpired, but he probably stopped her for money and she ignored him.

Julie and I were paralysed with fear. Suddenly the man yelled out, 'Suck my dick!' and started unzipping his fly. W started screaming. We were in the middle of *Irréversible*.

We were still screaming but I was covering my eyes. We could hear the sound of pissing. Whatever happened I did not want to see his crusty derro penis because I knew that would be an image I'd never be able to erase from my mind.

'Fuck this', said Julie, and swerved the car around the man, negotiated her way through the red light and took off down the road. Full credit to Julie that she managed not only to remove us from the situation but also had the ability to drive home.

After we had checked that each other was okay we drove home in silence. I asked Julie if she wanted to come in for some coffee but she said no, she just wanted to go home. I didn't blame her. I felt as though I had been beaten up. Totally defeated.

I felt as though I had been molested all weekend. I was exhausted. But the flashing derro did help me resolve one thing. I wouldn't get a gun. Given how anxious and vulnerable we felt after *Irréversible,* if I had a gun and the derro yelled out 'suck my dick', I would have gotten out of the car and killed him.

Chapter 27
Julie decides to seduce Douglas at the Bastille Day Ball

Love

Avoir les atomes crochus	To hit it off
Avoir le béguin pour	To have a crush on
Avoir un faible pour	To have a soft spot for
Avoir quelqu'un dans la peau	To have someone under your skin
être fou de	To be mad about
Vivre d'amour et d'eau fraiche	To live on love alone

For someone who is quite shy, when it came to potential love interests Julie had moments of real forcefulness. She was so assertive she was almost like someone else. One of those moments was when we were booking our tickets to the Bastille Day Ball.

Although we attended a lot of glamorous functions as part of our work, a ball was something quite different. It was a chance to dress up, eat beautiful food and dance. The Bastille Day Ball was another thing altogether. It was all the romance and glamour—and it was French.

Julie had by this stage become convinced that Douglas could be the Great French Romance. Only once had I commented on this remarkable turn of events.

'What, now that Laurant is out of the picture, Douglas has suddenly become hot?' I asked her at the French Film Festival while we were waiting for a film to start.

'I always thought he was hot!' she said defensively.

'No you didn't,' I teased, 'you said he was like a *frère*'.

'Well, that doesn't prove anything!' Julie insisted. 'You can still have the hots for a frère!'

Silence.

'Oh, no you can't', she added sheepishly as the lights went down.

Now that Julie had made up her mind about exactly where her true feelings belonged, she decided that the Bastille Day Ball was when she was going to get Douglas. We knew that Douglas was going to be there because he told us when we booked, but knowing that he was going to be there wouldn't necessarily mean that he would even talk to us. No, Julie needed him to be on the same table.

There was no way we could scam our way onto the same table as Douglas, we decided. We'd just have to ask him straight out. Which wouldn't be too difficult, we figured. Since our conversation with him at the film festival we were kind of friends—well, we had crossed over from being students who talk about school, to people who talk about their lives.

When we arrived, though, Douglas wasn't there, only Benjamin. Oh well, too bad I thought, and continued to the classroom. But Julie had stopped at the desk and was talking to Benjamin.

'We're going to the ball and I was wondering if the tables have been decided yet?'

'Ah, I don't think so,' said Benjamin, 'but you can request a table, like a French-speaking table, or if you have some friends who are also going'.

'Well, we want to be on a young table', said Julie, 'with young people. Like Douglas'.

My jaw almost hit the floor.

'I don't know if Douglas is going', replied Benjamin.

'He is,' said Julie firmly, 'we're friends with Douglas'.

'Okay', said Benjamin.

'We know him and he knows us', stressed Julie.

'Okay, I'll write it down', said Benjamin, grabbing a pen.

Julie leaned over the counter. 'That's Douglas yes? Doug-las … great'.

I couldn't imaging what Benjamin was going to say to Douglas, but Julie didn't seem too worried. In fact she looked positively proud of herself. I was pretty pleased too. Julie was going to get together with Douglas at the Bastille Day Ball. But before that happened, I was going to make another trip to Paris.

Chapter 28
Taxi cab revelations

The future

Formulation: - *ai*

                 - *as*

Infinitif +   - *a*

                 - *ons*

                 - *ez*

                 - *ont*

Irregular verbs:		
Aller (to go)	*j'irai, nous irons*
Avoir (to have)	*j'aurai, nous aurons*
Être (to be)	*je serai, nous serons*
Faire (to do)	*je ferai, nous ferons*
Pouvoir (to be able to)	*je pourrai, nous pourrons*

Once again, circumstances conspired and sent me on another trip to Paris. Liz, my sister, had taken a three-month leave of absence from the embassy to do an internship at the International Tribunal for the Former Yugoslavia in The Hague in the Netherlands. My mum was at the house in Ireland and she was planning on going to the Netherlands to visit Liz. Neither of us had ever been to the Netherlands and having Liz there was the perfect opportunity. Of course, Paris is only a stone's throw away from The Hague (well, by Australian standards anyway) so I emailed Alison, a friend of Liz's from the embassy, and she told me I was welcome to stay with her.

I met Alison during my last visit to Paris, and to me, she was someone who had the perfect handle on Paris. She was originally from Melbourne but had spent most of her life travelling and working, the closest thing to putting down roots being her current stay in Paris.

Alison loved Paris, but not because it was useful in inflating her ego. She never adopted an air of arrogance because she was at home in Paris, and she never expressed any notion that by living in Paris she was so much better than her other friends. She adored the French food and the culture and the fact that being there meant that she was close to other European cities, which she could visit.

Although many people, like my friend Butterfly Butcher, have felt defeated by Paris, that could never happen to Alison. Sure, she encountered problems with living in a foreign city and she knew that the French are often cold and unwilling to help. The difference was, she never equated those problems with the city of Paris. They were just problems, and for all the hard times, living in Paris was a lot of fun for a single, sophisticated woman.

I arrived at Charles de Gaulle at 6.30am and after twenty-four hours on a plane I was too tired for nervousness. The taxi driver didn't speak a word of English so I was forced to speak French. Getting into the cab, I wasn't too worried. I had Alison's address, so in the worst case (not being understood) he would always know where to take me. Besides, I was too tired to even think about things like verb conjugations, sentence structure and vocabulary. I'll do what I can and that's all, I thought.

On the Périphérique, the highway that circles Paris and separates the city from the *banlieu* (the suburbs), traffic ground to a halt. 'I'm sorry', the driver, a young black man, said. 'It's because of the strike.'

'What is it with the French and strikes?' I asked.

The driver laughed. 'I don't know', he shrugged.

'I think the French just love a revolution!' I said.

'Yes, yes, yes!' The driver chuckled. 'Vive la révolution!'

He wanted to know all about Australia and gushed with praise of how friendly he thought Australians were, how beautiful the country is, and how it is his dream to one day visit the country.

'I was a little worried that the French people might not like Australians anymore', I told him. 'Because we supported the invasion of Iraq ...'

'No, no, no.' The driver shook his head. 'We see the news on the television, and all the people protesting. We know Australians don't want to go to war, but sometimes the politicians don't listen. It is the same in every country, even France.'

As we crawled along the Périphérique, the driver asked, 'Why can you speak French?'

'Well, I can't speak it very well, just a bit!' I laughed.

The driver turned around. 'But you are speaking French', he looked puzzled. 'Not a bit …'

'Well, I'm learning it, and I watch a lot of French cinema … I try!'

The taxi driver looked triumphant. 'Never say you speak a little French—you speak French!' He seemed extremely pleased with this revelation. Every few minutes he would turn around and announce, 'You speak French!'

And I realised I could. Once I had decided not to bother worrying about grammar, sentence construction, vocabulary and correct pronunciation, it was as though I was set free. It was like my mind had suddenly opened up and given me access to everything I had learnt over the past two years.

Everything we talked about—Australia, France, the war in Iraq, my sister and his family—there was just not one topic of conversation that was out of my grasp. Okay, my speaking was probably very dodgy, and I knew I had a shocking accent, but I was understood.

It was really great to see Alison again. We were both talking so much. She made me a coffee while I had a shower and got changed. She had to go to work and I had appointments to keep, so we didn't have a long chat.

I worked out how to get to l'Opéra while I was having a coffee. Although my confidence in the language was peaking there was one thing that I was dreading: the Metro.

No matter how much I tried to block it from my head, *Irréversible* kept forcing itself into my thoughts. While I was zipping around Paris on my last visit with my new Paris Personality, I thought my fear of the city had disappeared. Now, I suddenly wasn't feeling as confident. Paris was not a friendly place and the Metro wasn't safe.

Like my previous trip I had interviews to do and stories to follow up and the only way to get to them was via the Metro. Plus, I knew that I would never get over *Irréversible* if I didn't face my fear.

At least my conversation with the taxi driver had built up my confidence and I felt that I would be able to make myself understood. When I arrived at the Metro Dupleix, I saw an American couple struggling to make themselves understood by the ticket seller and I was able to step in and speak to him for them.

Yet, making this first voyage on the Metro went without a hitch, and I didn't even feel that nervous. I just kept telling myself that I had as much of a right to be there as anyone—kind of like I owned the Metro.

But the truth was, once I was on the Metro, I didn't need to reassure myself that much. It was bright daylight, there were people everywhere, and no-one looked all that threatening. The only thing even resembling a derro that I saw, were those people who go from carriage to carriage, singing along to taped music and asking for money—and they were more irritating than anything. Even though it went without incident, that trip on the Metro was significant. I had walked through the gates terrified, because of my lack of confidence but mainly thanks to *Irréversible*, yet I walked through the gates regardless.

At my first stop, the perfumerie Fragonard, I met with the marketing manager and he took me through the press pack, which explained the history, philosophy and product range of Fragonard. On a professional level I find that the French are most serious and cold. Jean was no exception. As soon as he gave me the pitch and the media kit I was out of there.

Later that day I headed back to BMG. On the Metro I had to correspond twice but again I managed that without a hitch. I remembered where BMG was so that wasn't a problem either. Last year when I was there, Valérie came down to the foyer to meet me, but this time when the receptionist phoned to let her know that I was here, she told her to send me up.

I caught the elevator up to fifth floor and Valérie was there to meet me. At first she didn't recognise me because of my long hair. We went into the international office—it was a little warmer and more crowded than Fragonard. Valérie introduced me to another woman and the three of us chatted about music and their holidays—they were both very nervous about their forthcoming trips to Bali.

After I left BMG I headed home. On the way, I stopped at Franprix, the local supermarket and picked up some cold meats, salads and cakes. I watched a bit of television and read a bit and then I went to bed.

It was my first day in Paris and I had understood virtually everything that had been said to me, and had made myself understood also. It was the first time I really began to believe that I could speak French.

★★★★

Julie was laughing her head off. 'Margie', she said. 'You are reading too much into it!'

'Then why are you laughing?' I demanded.

'It's your voice! You sound so frightened! You're being silly. She's just being nice, and I think you will have a wonderful time with *women just like you!*'

I hoped Julie was right but I had my suspicions. Juliette, the editor of *Paris Woman Journal,* had responded with enthusiasm to my email announcing my upcoming visit to Paris. A little too much enthusiasm.

'I hope you don't mind but I have organised a lunch party in your honour', she wrote. 'I have invited some women who are very excited to meet you. You will like them; they are just like you …'

The fact was, I had never met Juliette and she had never met me. Professionally, our relationship was mutually beneficial, but I didn't know a whole lot about her personally. She occasionally spoke of her husband and son, but she also regularly commented on how beautiful I was (she got that idea from the very touched-up editor's letter on gURLpool) and signed her emails with kisses. Sure, her magazine was very classy and professional, but I knew more than anyone about the reality behind glamorous women's magazines.

Most people don't know it, but there's a Club Med right in the centre of Paris. Stepping out at Bercy Village I could have been walking into a provincial village—or Disneyland. Bercy Village is a new area, designed in the old style. There are streets of tiny shops and restaurants and cobblestone streets. It was a beautiful day, the temperature was in the high twenties.

Amongst this old-style French village is the ultra-modern Club Med World, a restaurant and bar—but it also has a climbing wall and an area for learning circus tricks. So you can have a meal or a drink, have a dance, and at the same time watch people rock-climbing or learning the flying trapeze.

Juliette met me at the station. Julie was right. There was nothing at all sinister about Juliette. She was just a friendly person. She was anxious to know what I thought of Bercy Village and what I fancied eating and how I was enjoying my stay in Paris. My *Irréversible*-inspired panic about Paris had just made me suspicious, I thought.

She said we had to meet her friend Maxine there. When Maxine showed up, Juliette introduced us. 'I know you', said Maxine. 'I don't think so', I said. 'I only arrived yesterday.' It turned out that Maxine was the girl at Fragonard who took me to the marketing office.

We had lunch at a restaurant in Bercy Village, sitting out in the sun. Another friend of Juliette's joined us. She was only twenty-six, but ran her own really interesting business. When I told Alison about it, she knew it because of all the press it was receiving. Urban Safari organise tours for groups via SMS messages. Everyone meets at a certain place and they all receive text messages to go to the next place where someone is waiting for them. The messages are a bit cryptic so teamwork is required, and each tour has a theme, like perfume or gastronomy.

We had salmon and salad for lunch and it was just lovely sitting out in the sunshine. I didn't feel like a guest. I felt like I was sitting in a Paris restaurant with my French friends. Then I realised I was.

After lunch, Juliette, Maxine and I went shopping at Les Halles. It was as crowded as I have ever seen it and because it was so hot it wasn't the most ideal of shopping conditions. I wanted to buy a book so we went to fnac. I couldn't find anything that interested me, plus I was hot and frazzled. But Juliette was right onto it.

'I know exactly the book you will love!' she said, returning a few moments later with the newly released *Qui a tué Daniel Pearl*. I could have cried with delight, had I not been so surprised. I have had a long-time fascination with foreign correspondents, and over the years have collected books written by journalists who have travelled to war-torn countries. I had been particularly affected by the murder in Pakistan of Daniel Pearl, a journalist for the *Wall Street Journal,* because I had been following his career and work.

Juliette bought the book for me, but my gratitude extended further than having been given a present. Not only had this stranger organised a lunch especially for me, she somehow even knew my taste. I have always thought the French were extremely insular and unmoving, but Juliette dispelled that myth completely.

★★★★

That evening I left Alison's apartment and stayed at a tiny hotel right across the street from her building. It was a decision based on my love of watching the Cannes Film Festival and my need for a television, but had I not stayed in a hotel, I would most certainly have missed my flight out of Paris. I knew the Cannes awards ceremony was being televised that night, which would have been the perfect night in for me, except for one problem—Alison didn't have a TV. Add to that the fact that Alison was expecting her flatmate home from a holiday in Italy that night, and I knew the only solution was to book into a hotel.

I love television and I cannot understand how people live without it. How do people leave the house in the morning without knowing exactly the state of the world? Perhaps my need to constantly be updated on the news is because I work in the media, but then television haters would argue I could always read the paper. More likely it's because I love a good story, and it doesn't matter if that story is a one-hour rerun of *Dallas* or a three-minute article on the nightly news. This night in Paris, though, the only story was what was happening in Cannes.

Sitting on my bed in my pajamas, smoking, I caught the end of the news, and that's when I learnt about the *grève.* Strikes are a way of life in Paris, memorable because of the sheer number, and because people just seem to accept them, and because they begin like clockwork with the first rays of summer sun.

Les grèves are such a part of life that at the end of the news, just before the weather, the news service features a *grève* diary, a list of what strikes are scheduled for what days in the coming week. And the next day—the day I was due to fly out to Ireland—there was going to be a taxi strike.

Quickly I threw on some clothes and ran down to reception where I explained to the concierge that in the morning I was going to need a taxi to get me to the airport.

'Don't worry', he assured me. 'My friend has a taxi. I will call him and he will take you.'

'What about the *grève?*' I asked.

'Don't worry, my friend will look after you.'

The next morning I dragged my cases down to reception and settled my account. 'Just sit in here and my friend will be here soon', said the concierge.

Just as the taxi pulled up, Ky called me on my mobile. The concierge and his friend were struggling to put my luggage in the boot, while fighting off frantic Parisians who had spied one of the only taxis on the road in Paris. I was trying to help them, alternating my conversation with Ky, instructions to the concierge, and dissuasions to people trying to steal my taxi.

When I was all packed up and ready to go, I said goodbye to the concierge. 'Thank you so much!' I cried. 'You are so kind! Thank you!' I blurted out in appreciation.

'What's wrong?' exclaimed Ky on the other end of the phone.

'Nothing', I answered, surprised.

'Why were you yelling at that man? What did he do to you?'

My forceful, strong expressions had made Ky, who had not one word of French, think I was abusing the concierge. In reality, I was being about as nice to him as a stranger could be. Not only had my language hit the mark, it occurred to me, the way I delivered it had, too.

Chapter 29
Margie visits the 'poor man's France'

At the post office

Envoyer une lettre	To send a letter
La boîte aux lettres	Mailbox
Affranchir la lettre	Put stamps on
Affranchissement par avion	Postage by air

Mum met me at the airport in Dublin and we spent a week at her house in the west of Ireland. Then we flew together to Holland to visit Liz. We stayed in The Hague for a few days, but as Liz had to work, we decided to take off on our own and visit a place neither of us had been to before—Belgium. While I was excited about travelling to a new country, the idea of Belgium didn't exactly thrill me. In my mind I was a France girl—what could the poor man's France offer? Plus, I was enjoying spending time in a country where I wasn't expected to understand the language and where the people were very laid back.

Because we were only going to be away for four days, we just took our day packs and left most of the luggage at The Hague. Mum and I caught the tram to the central station and then the train to Antwerp. There were a couple of anxious moments because the train we were told to catch didn't have Antwerp written anywhere on it, but the conductor soon moved through and told us where to get off. We needn't have been worried; the conductor was unexpectedly helpful.

Our first taste of Belgian beer came a few minutes after establishing that we were, in fact, in Belgium. Getting off the train at Antwerp, we were surprised to see all the signs were still in Dutch and to hear everyone was speaking in what we thought was Dutch. Later we cottoned on to the fact that the language of Flanders is Flemish, a form of Dutch, but not before ashamedly consulting our map to double-check that we were in fact in Belgium.

I was surprised that Flemish was still spoken in parts of Belgium. Belgium, by all accounts, is a poor man's France, and even the poorest of men in France refuse to speak any language other than French.

I was a little nervous about travelling to a French-speaking country with Mum. Sure, my confidence had been exceptionally high in Paris, and I had spoken the language without bother. But now I was with my mum—someone I did not want to look foolish in front of, and someone who I did not want to be disappointed in me. So, in a way, it was a relief not to know the language.

Across the road from the station was a small restaurant with a terrace called Des Arts. We were greeted by what we assumed was a waiter, but what appeared to be a weightlifter on his lunchbreak; complete with singlet, which revealed arms like tree trunks, baggy cotton pants and hair cropped to his skull, except for a long fringe. He plonked the menus in front of us and disappeared into the restaurant.

Yep, I thought, there's the French attitude.

Despite his appearance, the waiter was extremely friendly and eager to help. 'What rabbits eat', he explained with a demonstration. Ah, carrots. 'Yellow sauce', he answered, confirming my suspicions that curry was actually curry.

One thing he was insistent upon was that we order De Konnick beer, which is brewed in Antwerp. De Konnick is a red, flavoursome beer, both sweet and bitter. Like our waiter, it is meaty enough to be remembered but, unlike our waiter, it is light.

After catching our connecting train at Antwerp, it was only another hour to Brugges. When we arrived we caught the bus to the main square, Market Square, where the tourist information centre is. The first thing we noticed was what a beautiful place Brugges is—it's a tiny, medieval city with cobbled streets, stone buildings and many lovely squares. The second thing we noticed was the shopping. The streets were lined with gorgeous boutiques and food shops. Mum and I looked at each other with amazement. Why had we never heard of this place before? This was heaven!

We got off the bus and turned the corner into Market Square and were left speechless by the amazingly intricate Romanesque architecture on the buildings and all the terrace restaurants in front of them. The tourist information office gave us accommodation listings, so it was just a case of choosing the hotels we wanted and asking the staff to phone them for us.

The hotel we got couldn't have been more central, in a street off Market Square. As we were walking down the street with our luggage, a waiter appeared and offered to give us directions. We showed him the name and he not only pointed out where it was, he took us there. Sure, it was only a few doors up, but it was more than he needed to do.

We weren't able to book in straightaway, so we went for a small stroll around the town, and when the waiter saw us—still with our luggage half an hour later—he asked us why we still had our bags. When we explained, he looked surprised. 'Why didn't you ask me to hold them for you?' he asked.

Like an old friend.

Naturally we went back to Strijdershuis for dinner. It was beginning to cool down so it was lovely on the terrace. Mum was served an incredibly light and fluffy omelette and I had a bowl of salmon pasta. Our beer for the night, on our waiter's recommendation, was Straffe Henrik, which means Strong Henry and which is brewed in Brugge. Although smelling strongly of hops, it had only the subtlest of flavours, and was served before our meal with a bowl of radishes and pretzels. The best beer for cooling down and relaxing.

It might have the reputation of being the poor man's France, but we soon fell in love with Belgium and the wonderfully warm people who welcomed us into their big Belgium family. The guy at reception told us that he lived in Brugges and gave us a map on which he marked all his favourite places. Our room was in the attic and was very cute with its A-frame ceiling, wood panels and roof window.

Tuesday morning we woke up covered in mozzie bites. It was way too hot to sleep with the windows shut and of course none of the windows had flywire on them. The mixture of lots of canals and the heat made for mozzie heaven. The fact that the church bells rang out every morning at exactly eight o'clock meant that we didn't get the chance to sleep in, so we went to the breakfast room for what was, for us, an unusual breakfast. It was a buffet and some of the items we chose were egg and crabmeat salad, toast, ham and sardines. Oh, and a slice of cake to finish.

We spent the morning shopping and then headed towards a place that our concierge described as 'where old nuns live'. We weren't sure if he meant it was a sort of retirement village for old nuns, or whether it was a disused nunnery. We concluded that it was most likely the retirement option, because of the 'Silence' signs everywhere. It was a gorgeous walled estate with tiny little gardens and tiny little houses. Next to it was a park with a lake in the middle that our concierge assured us was a love lake. 'Throw in a coin and make a love wish and that wish will always come true', he said. 'Always?' I asked skeptically. 'Always', he replied.

After tossing a coin (strangely, Mum tossed two) we stopped and had another beer and did our assessment. We were pretty tired by this stage, but we wanted to check out the museum while it was still open. The great thing about Brugges is that everything is so close. We walked through the museum, which contained household, religious and community pieces from the region. The mansion it was housed in was equally spectacular, especially the chapel room. The mansion was built right next to the church and there was a special room where the family could attend mass without leaving their house—the room opened up into the cathedral.

The fact that everyone spoke English in Belgium helped remove some of the stress of travelling, but while it was very similar to France, the atmosphere was infinitely friendlier and more welcoming. I didn't think about needing to protect myself at all.

We stayed in Belgium for a week in total, leaving Brugges to go into the Ardenne and Brussels. When we left Flanders and moved deeper into Belgium I knew there was no avoiding it—I would have to speak French in front of Mum. At first it was just at the railway station and I doubt Mum would have been particularly impressed by my *Je voudrais deux billets à Namur, s'il vous plaît'*. But when we arrived in the ancient city it was up to me to organise a hotel and get us there.

The tourist information centre was at the station and I managed to establish very quickly that all we had to do was look at the guide, choose a hotel and they would call and book it. I stammered a little, but the woman was patient and soon our hotel was booked.

We were tired and it was late, so we decided to catch a taxi. We got into the first cab and I showed the driver the map. We drove away from the city centre and began climbing the winding road up the cliff face. The driver asked me some questions about where we were from and what we were doing in Belgium—the usual questions. By this stage I had no problem answering because I had answered the same questions many times before.

Although Mum never said anything to the effect of 'Wow, your French is great!' her confidence in my French was evidenced by the fact that she asked me to translate all the time. And I mean *all the time*. In restaurants, shops, asking directions, even asking a guide to tell us the history of the city's ancient citidel—and then to translate what the guide said back to her in English.

I was happy to oblige for the most part, pleased to be able to practise the language, and pleased to be indispensable to Mum. But as the trip progressed and travelling took its toll, it became more difficult.

It had been a long day. We started early, catching a bus to an ancient tiny town about an hour from Namur, which was situated on a hillside deep in the Ardenne. It was a pretty town that existed alongside the magnitude of the citadel. After wandering around, we quickly ate lunch and caught a bus to another town and another citadel, which was the crossroads for several rail lines and bus routes.

Once there, we had to decide where we would go next. The towns and citadels of the Ardenne were all beginning to look the same, so we were looking for something different. 'You know,' said Mum slowly, looking at the map, 'Luxembourg is only an hour or so from here …'

'Mmmm', I replied. 'Do you want to go to Luxembourg?'

'Why not?' Mum's eyes lit up. 'Let's go there for dinner!'

'To another country for dinner?'

'Why not?'

So we did. The next train for Luxembourg left within the hour and we were on it. We spent what was left of the afternoon doing a walking tour of the tiny principality and having dinner at the Luxembourg Pizza Hut. Tiny in size Luxembourg may be, we discovered, but just about everything was huge in price.

By nine o'clock we were back at the station, physically and mentally exhausted. I booked our tickets home, found our platform and plonked myself down on the bench to wait for the train. All the trips we had taken had been less than an hour, but we had travelled further away from our base at Namur, and it wouldn't take us less than three hours to get home. We still had a long night ahead of us.

'Margie,' said Mum, studying the train map, 'go up and ask the ticket man what time the train arrives in Dinan'.

'It took an hour to get here', I responded. 'I imagine it would take us about the same to get back.'

'But it might be a faster or slower train. If it's slower, we'll miss the connecting train and we'll have to wait for another.'

There was no way I was moving and certainly no way I was going to attempt to explain my request in French, especially as it seemed so unnecessary. 'Mum, knowing how fast or slow the train is will not help us in any way. If we have to wait, we have to wait. I just don't want to speak to him.'

'It's easy', Mum explained. 'Just say *le train*—then whatever the word is for "will"—*arrive à quelle heure …*'

That was it—I burst into tears. Mum was mortified and quickly abandoned the whole idea of me asking the ticket seller any question. I am exhausted, I explained. It wasn't that I couldn't work out how to ask what time the train will arrive at its destination, I just couldn't bear to think about it. A week of speaking non-stop French was exhausting. 'Sometimes,' I explained, 'I'm just so sick of speaking French'.

We staggered into the foyer of the converted brick nunnery, which was the hotel, well after dinner had been served, cleared and the kitchen closed. 'Please', I begged the stout concierge, who had told us when we checked in that he spoke no English. 'We need a coffee desperately.'

'The kitchen is closed', said another man who was standing behind him shaking his head.

'Go to your room.' The concierge smiled warmly.

A few minutes later there was a knock on the door and I opened it to the concierge, who was carrying a large tray laden with coffee, milk and chocolate. I felt like I was about to burst into tears again. 'I give you extra chocolate.' He smiled as he put the tray on the table. *'Bonne nuit!'* And he left.

I could hardly wait to tell Julie. Don't be put off by the fact that Douglas is from Belgium, be happy about it. Belgium, I texted her, is like France, but without the bad attitude.

Chapter 30
Classes become a piece of gâteau

The war in Iraq

Des armes de destruction massive	Weapons of mass destruction
La zone d'exclusion aérienne	No fly zone
Nations Unies	United Nations
Le Golfe Persique	The Persion Gulf
Le Conseil de Sécurité	The Security Council

Although I had been back in Australia for two days, my French experience was not yet over. While French film has a big audience in Australia, music from France had never really taken off. Petrol Records was trying to change that.

Paris: the sex, the city and the music was the new CD release from Petrol Records, compiled and sequenced by French-born DJ Jean-Francois Ponthieux. It was an unexpected mix of smooth and harmonious and unashamedly electronic dance music, from some lesser-known, but very happening French artists. The week I returned to Australia, I learnt that gURLpool had organised for me to interview Ponthieux.

If the world music compilations we've been fed to date are anything to go by, French music can be summed up in a few words: Edith Piaf, Serge Gainsbourg, Brigitte Bardot. Yet, for those who have spent any time in the city, this music is to France what Banjo Paterson is to Australia—part of the cultural heritage, but not really representative of what is going on at the moment.

I met with the handsome Jean-Francois Ponthieux at Blue Tongue, a trendy bar in Elwood. He was interested in my recent trip and pleased to talk with an Australian who was *au fait* with modern French music.

'Is it possible to re-create the whole vibe of a city in one CD?' I began by asking.

'No. I could have gone on', he replied. 'This is just a snapshot. This is just for like a party in your living room with your friends, you know?'

I decided to share with Jean-Francois my take on French music. 'You've got one group of singers, like Johnny Hallyday, who have been around for decades and who continue to sell records. It's like once you're a music sensation in France, you continue to be for the rest of your life. Then you have another group of younger, funkier musicians. There seems to be quite a divide ...'

'That is quite correct and there is a reason for this', he explained. 'There is a government who says that forty per cent of the broadcasting has to be French language music, and there is a great variety of songs from artists like Johnny Hallyday, so they play it. And the people have been brainwashed. That is why a lot of the electronic music, guys like Rubin Steiner, are big overseas but not so much known in their own country. That's why rap and hip-hop are so big in France—because they wanted something that was in and was also in French.'

'Why do you think everything French is so popular in Australia?' I asked.

'Well, sometimes I think it isn't. When I came to Australia first there was a nuclear bomb exploded in the Pacific and there were posters of Chirac everywhere and stickers about the French. For a little while I told everyone I was from Belgium! When France didn't join the war [against Iraq] people were very happy I was French. It was the first time I felt it was okay to be French.

'But I think it is like, what you say, the grass is always greener. I think Australia is a very young country. It is gradually building its own country. But sometimes I think there is a cultural envy of some places around the world.'

'I think Paris has a kind of false mythology ... fashion, for example', I said. 'France is seen as a fashion leader but I can't see anything new or exciting coming out of France. Is it the same with music?'

'That is very true', he agreed. 'I think sometimes when a country is a leader in something it stops, it doesn't move forward. We've seen it with wine. France used to produce great wines and it didn't progress, so now countries like Australia and South America have overtaken them. Music is absolutely the counter-example of what is happening in fashion. In France there was no electronic music and it wasn't played on the radio, so people actually went out and said, what can we create? And now it is very innovative and exciting.'

On returning from France I noticed that two things had changed with my French. The most important was that I was no longer panicked when I was asked a question and was expected to respond. Until now, when I was asked a question what would run through me head was, 'Hell, how do I say this?' Now I was unfazed. I knew that I would be able to put across what I meant, even if it was in a roundabout way. And it was amazing how it freed my mind. Verbs and nouns were all suddenly at my disposal.

And at long last I was able to understand pretty much everything that was said to me. It was the final corner and I think our new teacher Celine was largely responsible for the turning. Julie and I had now completed our entire French course, from Beginners to Advanced, and the only option available to us was Conversation and Grammar classes, which were designed for French-speakers who wanted to refine or practise their skills.

Celine's speech was extremely clear to begin with, but her skill was in the way she would deliver it. She would say a sentence, not particularly slowly, but clearly, and then repeat key words. It wasn't obvious that she was doing it, but she was making herself heard in the most effective way.

By the time I returned to Australia I knew that I could speak French—and it showed in my first class back. Julie had to work, so it was necessary for me to go by myself. Normally the thought of going to class by myself would have freaked me out, but my confidence was high. And I had enough of the Paris Personality to see me through.

Celine was clearly happy to see me. She asked me about my trip. She also asked me about all the strikes, because the class had been watching the news bulletins and talking about them while I was away.

The conversation for class was based around magazine advertisements. Celine had ripped some out of a magazine and we talked about the images that were presented and why they were used. Then we were divided up into two groups and given the instructions to create our own advertisement, which we would then present to the other group, who were the 'clients'.

Our group consisted of me, Pierre and a woman Julie and I named Hyacinth Bouquet. She was a stereotypical middle-aged, middle-class English woman, complete with permed hair and floral shirts, which she no doubt referred to as blouses. In the other group were a grumpy grey-haired woman and two younger women I had never seen before. I was hyped on jet-lag induced adrenaline so I immediately took over.

'We need a star', I started. 'What about Monica Bellucci? She's every-where in France at the moment.'

The others agreed. Under my animated and forceful instruction we constructed an ad for a portable. Monica Bellucci is in bed, draped in a sheet, speaking on the phone. In the background is Vincent Cassel. All we needed was a slogan.

'Plus désirable que Vincent Cassel?' offered Pierre humbly.

'Parfait!' Hyacinth and I cheered.

I presented our campaign to the others. They didn't have much to say, except for Grumpy Grey-haired Woman. She wanted to know why we chose Monica Bellucci.

'She's very, very popular at the moment', I explained. 'She's on all the magazines and newspapers, because she hosted Cannes.'

'No she didn't', scoffed Grumpy Grey-haired Woman.

'Yes she did', I responded, a little bit puzzled.

'No, she didn't', insisted Grumpy Grey-haired Woman.

'Yes she did', interjected Celine.

'What, the whole thing?' Grumpy Grey-haired Woman looked at us like we were a couple of imbeciles.

'Yes!' I said.

'Well, I don't understand how she could host the whole thing', she scoffed to show that this conversation was over.

Then it was time for the other team to present their ads. They chose a holiday in Tahiti. A mermaid was sitting on a beach and the slogan read, 'Tahiti, the perfect holiday'.

My question was, would the ad appeal to women as well as to men, to which they hummed and hahhed until conceding that it wouldn't. 'Are the clients happy?' asked Celine, smiling.

'No, not really', I said. The class laughed. 'It's just a little boring and not original.'

Well, it was how I felt, but under normal circumstances I knew I wouldn't have been so blunt. I knew that the Paris Personality had not yet worn off.

Chapter 31
The night of the Bastille Day Ball arrives

Adverbs
- adjectives modify a noun: *une robe bleue*
- adverbs modify a verb or adjective: *c'est absolument ça*

Adjective	Adverb
final / finale (final)	*finalement* (finally)
fort / forte (strong)	*fortement* (strongly)
parfait / parfaite (perfect)	*parfaitement* (perfectly)
extrême (extreme)	*extrêmement* (extremely)
facile (easy)	*facilement* (easily)
rapide (rapid)	*rapidement* (rapidly)
naturel / naturelle (natural)	*naturellement* (naturally)

I hardly had time to unpack my cases before it was the night of the Bastille Day Ball. Given that the Bastille Day Ball was also the night that Julie decided she was going to seduce Douglas, some effort went into her presentation. Months before, she had found some extremely sheer gorgeous blue and green material, which she had bought without a real purpose in mind. Now that she had one, she set to work. She scoured fashion magazines and found a Versace dress she felt was perfect—and from that picture, made a pattern and the dress. It was fitted and had a plunging neckline and no back at all.

Having no conquest on my agenda, choosing my dress for the ball was a little less stressful. It did require an entire day at a shopping centre though, a fact that I think was unrealised by Kieran, my eleven-year-old godson, who eagerly volunteered to go with me.

After hours of trying on dresses that weren't quite right, Kieran was irritable and I was disappointed. In the last store we visited I decided to forgo my prejudices and look in the bridal-wear section, in the hope that somewhere amongst the hot pink taffeta I might find something suitable. What caught my eye was a skirt. It had a small satin waistband from which flowed metres and metres of the finest black tulle. When I walked out of the dressing room, the exhausted Kieran almost jumped out of his chair. 'Margie!' he exclaimed. 'You look like a princess from a Disney movie.' I was sold.

Julie met me at my house and when I opened the door I gasped. She looked lovely in her dress and her hair was blow-waved straight and shiny. Of course all this grooming took some time and we were hideously late. Without wasting too much time gushing over each other, Lincoln drove us to the St Kilda Town Hall, which was less than five minutes away.

The tricolours were hanging from every flagpole on the town hall and French music was wafting through the doors as we drove up. Julie was noticeably nervous and had her fingers in her mouth the whole way.

The inside of the hall was gorgeous. The St Kilda Town Hall is one of the oldest buildings in Melbourne, with high ceilings and intricate designs on the walls and it had been decorated in red, white and blue. We signed in and the hostess told us which number table we were on. Making our way through the tables, we scoured the room for people who we might know, but saw no-one.

None of the other people on our table had arrived yet, so we sat down and waited. Every time a new group of people walked into the room, our eyes shot to the door to see if was Douglas. Eventually, a group of middle-aged men and women walked over to our table.

'Hello there!' one of the men cheerfully greeted us. 'Looks like we're sharing a table! My name's Martin.'

Martin was dressed in a cheap suit and what looked to be an even cheaper shirt and tie. His hair was slicked back, so he had obviously at least showered for the event. None of his friends looked any better and their wives, who were wearing what could only be described as floral summer dresses, were worse.

Julie looked distraught. 'Are you sure this is your table?' she asked Martin desperately. 'Number seventeen?'

'Yep', answered Martin and introduced his friends, who sat down.

'Wow', said one of the women, in awe. 'This place looks real classy ...' Her companions agreed.

'So, Martin', I began pleasantly, trying to lift Julie's spirits. 'Are you a student at the Alliance Française?'

'Heck no!' laughed Martin. 'Don't *parlez* a word of it myself. No, we work for a small plastics factory and sometimes we like to get together and do something a bit different, you know? We heard about this do and thought why the hell not?'

I could almost feel Julie hyperventilating.

A few minutes later it was announced that the buffet dinner was being served and we were directed to line up according to table number. The buffet consisted of fish, cold meats and salads. It looked a little disappointing, but by this stage I was starving. Julie soon discovered that she was going to remain starving—not one single salad had no meat and she is a vegetarian. With just a few dinner rolls on her plate, she headed back to the table where there was still no Douglas.

After dinner we moved into the room where the dance floor was. Julie's face lit up as we entered. It wasn't Douglas she was smiling at though, it was Benjamin.

This isn't the way it is supposed to go, I thought, panicking. I must keep Julie away from Benjamin. Benjamin sashayed into the room followed by about five girls. He was holding court and dancing with a different girl for every song. It wasn't long before he spotted the gorgeous Julie and zeroed in. While they were dancing I went over to the bar to get another drink and spotted Douglas, looking as funky as ever in a velvet suit and gold shirt.

'Douglas!' I exclaimed. 'We didn't think you were coming?'

'Oh I wanted to come earlier', he said. 'But it was so busy at the Alliance, I just could not leave earlier!'

'Well, find us later and we'll have a drink', I said.

Julie walked up and kissed Douglas and again made him assure us that he would find us later, which he did. He was obviously flustered.

Douglas had a lot of duties, from selling raffle tickets, to hosting and greeting people and helping Jean-Philippe officiate.

For someone who had just danced with Benjamin, Julie walked up to me looking a little stressed. But before I had a chance to ask her what was wrong, I was hit by an excruciatingly pungent acidic smell. I turned around and there was Benjamin standing next to me.

There was clearly something up with this guy. He smelt awful and he was sweating like he had just run a marathon. He looked dreadful. Not knowing what to say to him, I smiled and asked, 'So, whereabouts in France are you from Benjamin?'

'I am actually from Belgium', he slurred. 'But the French part of Belgium. I don't even think of myself as Belgian. I am more French than Belgian …'

You're more pathetic than anything, I wanted to mumble.

Benjamin didn't improve with the night. As he became more drunk he became more obnoxious and embarrassing. We ran into him and his entourage several times out the front of the building having a cigarette and every time he danced around singing Julie's name at the top of his voice. Julie was torn between being flattered and being embarrassed.

Every time we ran into Douglas he was busy, so we didn't have a chance to really talk much and Julie was certainly not presented with an opportunity to chat him up. Which wasn't to say we weren't out of his thoughts. Douglas held the bag containing the tickets during the raffle draw and as he walked up on stage for the draw, he found Julie and I and smiled and crossed his fingers theatrically.

Even so, our spirits lifted once Douglas and Benjamin arrived and we danced and drank and chatted for the rest of the night. We didn't win the door prize, which was a trip to Paris, and Julie didn't get to pick up Douglas but we did eventually have a fun night.

It was going to be interesting to see how our relationships with Douglas and Benjamin changed after the Bastille Day Ball. Douglas would be a little more familiar with us and Benjamin, we expected, probably wouldn't even remember us.

When we walked into the Alliance, Benjamin was the first to see us. His eyes instantly lit up, which was followed quickly by his mock hanging his head in shame. Oh, he remembered all right.

'Did you have a good time at the ball?' asked Benjamin.

'Yes, it was great', laughed Julie. 'You looked like you were having a good time. Did you go out afterwards?'

'We just went to my house', he said, looking sheepish. 'I went to bed at 4 am!'

Douglas also had a big smile on his face when he saw us. 'Hello.' he grinned, walking over. 'Did you have fun at the ball?'

'Yes', I said, changing the subject. 'Hey Douglas, do you speak Dutch?'

'Yes. Why?'

'I bought a book of comics in Holland and I don't know what it means ...' Douglas laughed. 'The thing is,' I continued, 'I think it might be disgusting and I am too embarrassed to ask anyone!'

In fact, I knew the comic book was disgusting and I was just trying to make conversation. In Holland, these comics were everywhere—they featured prominently in newspapers and took centre stage in bookstore displays. The comics featured two teenage boys called Fokke and Sukke, and the reason I purchased the book was not just as a souvenir, but because I was shocked that something with such blatant sexual references should be so mainstream.

I had everyone's attention. 'Bring it in', said Douglas.

'I've got it here', I replied. I pulled out the book and Douglas laughed.

'Put it this way,' he said, 'you wouldn't show this to a Dutch child'.

We must have been laughing loudly because at that moment Celine came out of the class and looked at us. We were already half an hour late, so we quickly said goodbye and went to our class. Even though we had made our way to Advanced Conversation and Grammar, and even with all the corners we had turned, that didn't mean we were now immune to humiliation. Julie and I called them Dumb Nights, and that night we both had simultaneous Dumb Nights.

One method Celine used to get us talking was to make a statement about something to do with France and ask us if the situation was the same in Australia. On this particular night we were discussing food and its relationship with culture.

We began by discussing the formality of meal service. Pierre and the new woman were talking about the relaxed nature of dining and the popularity of the buffet and the barbecue. Then we started on fast food.

'McDonald's is very popular here in Australia but not so much in France', said Celine.

'*Ah bon?*'

'Yes, in France the people did not like the hamburgers of McDonald's so it was necessary for them to introduce salads etcetera.'

'In Australia the young people love McDonald's', said Pierre. 'But the young people in France do not like McDonald's?'

And so it went on between Pierre and Celine, until Julie piped up with, '*Qu'est-ce que c'est McDonald's?*'

All heads turned to Julie and conversation stopped. '*Ce mot, McDonald's, je ne le connais pas ...*' she stumbled, aware that she might have said something foolish.

'McDonald's!' I said in English, laughing out loud. Julie burst out laughing at herself and the whole class followed. When we finally calmed down, Celine passed out the reading for homework. It was an article about the food habits of ancient civilisations. It was the end of class and I was beginning to zone out.

Next thing I knew Celine was looking at me. '*Comprenez-vous, blah blah blah?*'

'No', I said blankly. In truth I wasn't listening very well and the care factor was pretty low. Now the whole class was laughing again and this time I knew they were laughing at me. 'What?' I laughed.

'Jesus,' said Julie. 'You know, Jesus Christ!'

'That's it', smiled Celine. 'This class is over.'

Chapter 32
Margie starts working for a French tabloid

Adjectives in order of intensity
- *Supris* (surprised), *stupéfait* (astounded)
- *Intéressé* (interested), *passionné* (passionate)
- *Contrarié* (annoyed), *irrité* (irritated), *fâché* (angry)
- *heureux* (happy), *enchanté* (enchanted)

It took me several minutes of pondering before I was able to muster the courage to open the email. The sender was Editor and the subject was *The Connexion,* so the content of the email could be anything. In a click of the mouse I could be jumping for joy or cursing my bad luck.

During my last visit to Paris, Alison had given me a whole pile of English language French publications, knowing how I wanted to write for some. Most of them I knew, one had bought my champagne article. While she handed me the magazines, she kept one held to her chest.

'Now Margie,' she said with a sly look on her face, 'I want you to read this magazine. But I'm not going to give you my opinion. I want you to read it and then tell me what you think.' Then she chuckled quietly to herself.

Because I was so busy, I didn't get a chance to read *The Connexion* until my last night in Paris, when I was sitting in the hotel watching the Cannes Film Festival. Flipping through it I read a few of the headlines, 'Family Anger as Vegetarian Dies of Mad Cow Disease', 'Traffic Harms Male Fertility', 'Nose Job is TV Quiz Prize'. This was tabloid.

That in itself was surprising because European tabloids are generally on the more highbrow side of light entertainment. *Gala* and *Paris Match* are generally considered light reading, but they still contain their fair share of political and social issues. *The Connexion,* on the other hand, was unashamedly a tabloid, UK-style.

Yet, as I read the articles, I realised that rather than being pure trash and scandal, *The Connexion* was actually a very well written publication. It had a tone that suggested it could actually be mocking itself. Sure it was light news, but it tread the line between reportage and satire. It was written with an ever-so-slight mockery that I just love—and a style that I identified in my own writing.

I called Alison straightaway. 'I love *The Connexion*!' I cried.

She laughed. 'I knew you would; I love it too.'

'You know,' she added seriously, 'you should write for this paper'.

When I had arrived in Ireland, I immediately emailed the editor, introducing myself I gave her a brief description of my career and asked if I could submit an article for *The Connexion*. A few days later I received a response: 'Thank you for your interest in *The Connexion*. We have a group of journalists we work with and at the moment are not looking to add any more to our list …'

Not to be deterred, I put together a list of article suggestions and emailed the editor, with a note saying that if she was ever short of an article, I could write up one of the following ideas.

No response.

Now, three months later there was an email sitting in my inbox. I took a deep breath and opened it. The editor liked my story ideas and wanted me to write up two of them. And she wanted to call me to talk about future articles I could write for *The Connexion*. I was in.

Chapter 33
Douglas drops a bombshell

Verb drills: être (to be)
L'imparfait:
J'étais … (I was …)   *Nous étions …* (We were …)

Le futur:
Je serai … (I will be …)   *Nous serons …* (We will be …)

Le conditionnel:
Je serais … (I would be …)   *Nous serions …* (We would be …)

'Bonjour, Alliance Française, how may I help you?'
  'Hello, can I speak to Douglas, please?'
  'Yes, this is Douglas.'
  'Hi Douglas, this is Margaret Ambrose.'
  'Hi! How are you?'
  Shitting myself, that's how. I was sitting at home on a Friday morning and already I had smoked half a packet of cigarettes. I checked my emails and read the one from Julie: 'Don't forget to call Douglas. You promised.'
  Julie and I knew that Douglas was soon to return to Belgium and we calculated that the night before was the last time we would see him. Once he was gone, he would be out of our lives forever, we had no phone number and no email address. So we decided that when we saw him on the way to class we would ask him about his trip and casually ask for his email address.
  Well, that was the plan. And for the first few minutes the plan went smoothly: we parked, walked into the Alliance, said *'Bon soir!'* to Douglas

and Benjamin and then continued walking into class. Both Julie and I simultaneously lost our nerve. And the moment passed. By the time class had finished, Douglas had left for the night.

We were beside ourselves. On the drive home we contemplated our options. We could go into the Alliance on our day after work the next week and hope Douglas was still in the country, but there was a big chance that he would already have left, or we could ask one of the teachers or even Benjamin for his email address, but there was no guarantee they would give it to us.

'I could call him tomorrow', I blurted out.

'Yes,' said Julie. 'You have to do it. You must. Promise me you will do it?'

So I did.

'We didn't have a chance to speak to you last night,' I said, following the script Julie and I had concocted, 'and I just wanted to catch you before you went and say goodbye'.

'Oh, that's so nice,' said Douglas. 'But actually I will see you next Thursday. I don't leave until the following Sunday.'

'Oh, cool', I said. 'Well I guess we can say goodbye in person on Thursday then?'

'Yes,' said Douglas, and then he paused, 'maybe afterwards we can go for a drink?'

'Great!' I replied, trying to control my surprise and enthusiasm.

'We will go to the Dogs Bar, yes?'

'That sounds great. But we finish at eight and you work until seven, is that right?'

'That's okay, I will wait.'

As soon as I hung up the phone, I hammered out an email to Julie recounting the conversation word for word. 'If you paid me a million dollars every day for the rest of your life,' I wrote, 'you will never be able to repay me for what I have done for you ...'

Julie was almost half an hour late for class on the night of our big date with Douglas and she had clearly spent the extra time making herself gorgeous. She was wearing figure-hugging pants, stiletto heals and a tight black skivvy, and her straight hair was tied back in a ponytail.

We had, of course, coordinated our outfits in the week prior. Not knowing what look Douglas would prefer, we decided that she would go for sexy and I would go for sweet. I was wearing blue pastel pants and a baby-blue wrap top tied around the middle with a pink silk ribbon. After checking each other out and giving our nods of approval, we went to class.

Most of the class was a blur, but one thing I do remember is that both Julie and I excelled, propelled along by adrenaline and a sense that tonight was a special night. After packing up our books, Julie and I were the last ones in the class. 'Oh my God!' I cried. 'I'm too scared to go out there!'

'I know,' said Julie. 'Aggh!'

Eventually, we did make our way outside to the foyer. Behind the desk was Benjamin, attending to an inquiry. But no Douglas. We looked in the loungeroom, the kitchen and through all the classroom doors. No sign of him anywhere.

Our hearts sank. He's either forgotten or stood us up, we concluded despondently. At that moment Julie realised that her car was double-parked and there would be people trying to get out of the car park. We rushed out the front door and ran to the car park. It was a calamity. Four cars were trying to edge their way out with people directing them.

'Here's a suggestion for you', growled one man sarcastically to Julie. 'Move!'

By the time she had reversed backwards into the narrow alley and all the cars had managed to make their way out, Julie was rattled. I was just worried. We walked back into the Alliance and had another look around, but still no Douglas.

'Let's have a cigarette and then we'll go', I said, disappointed.

'I think he meant that he would meet us there', said Julie as we puffed.

'But he said he would wait!' I replied.

'Yeah, but maybe he meant he would meet us down there.'

'I dunno.' I was unconvinced.

'That was my first impression when I read your email', continued Julie, her spirits rising. 'I thought he meant that he was having a party at the Dogs Bar and that we shouldn't worry that we finish at eight because the party would still be going …'

'But it sounded like he meant it was going to be just us', I was beginning to think she might be right.

'Let's walk down there and just have a look', said Julie, standing up.

'Okay,' I said, 'but let's just have one last look inside first'.

We did and still no Douglas. Just as we were walking out the door, Benjamin approached us. 'Douglas was wondering if you would join him at the Dogs Bar for a drink', he said.

We walked out of the Alliance. 'See,' said Julie, 'he's down there with some people from the Alliance and he just got Benjamin to remind us where he was!' I had to admit she sounded right. As we walked down Acland Street, we saw Jean-Phillippe, the director of the Alliance Française, walk into the bar. 'See,' said Julie, 'even Jean-Phillippe is going'.

Even though we now knew that we hadn't been stood up, I was still a little disappointed that it wasn't going to be just the three of us like I had thought. When we walked into the Dogs Bar we saw Douglas sitting at a table with another guy. We walked over and said hi and he introduced us to the other guy, a marketing guy at Qantas.

'Do you want a drink?' I asked Julie. She nodded and we walked over to the bar. 'Should we go and sit with him?' I asked Julie nervously. 'Maybe he's keeping those seats for someone …'

'Of course', she said and walked back over. Qantas guy, who in my head I had already nicknamed Flying Kangaroo, excused himself and went to the bar. 'I am so sorry', Douglas said as we arrived at the table. 'I thought we would have a night to ourselves but he really wanted to say goodbye and this was the only time.' Julie had been wrong. We were the only ones invited.

I looked up. Jean-Philippe had appeared next to the table. 'Here', he said, pulling out a chair for Julie, 'you sit here next to Douglas'. He sat at the end of the table and pulled out a chair for me between him and Flying Kangaroo.

Flying Kangaroo hardly spoke but the conversation between Jean-Philippe, Douglas, Julie and me was easy. We talked about the Alliance, French, gossiped about the teachers and talked about Douglas leaving.

Douglas was paying me a lot of attention and was telling the others all about me.

'She went to The Hague', he told them. 'Her sister lives in Paris!' he said another time. I was surprised and flattered that he remembered so much about me, and thoroughly enjoyed talking to him.

'You should hear what she said,' he exclaimed. 'They were talking about Belgium ...'

'That was you?' shouted Jean-Philippe. Everyone laughed because my 'France without the bad attitude' comment I had made about Belgium had apparently become legendary around the Alliance.

'You are his goddess, do you know that?' asked Jean-Philippe. 'You are Douglas's goddess!' Well, I didn't mind that a bit.

After a while, Jean-Philippe swivelled around and started talking to me alone. 'What is it that you do?' he asked.

'I'm a journalist,' I replied, 'I work for a women's magazine'.

'What is it that you specialise in?' Was it just my imagination or was he moving closer?

'I'm the editor,' I said, 'I edit the whole magazine'.

'But you are so young for this position!' Jean-Philippe exclaimed. He leant over and touched my hair.

'I'm not as young as I look', I spluttered. 'I'm thirty-four ...'

'Do you have a family?' he asked, looking into my eyes.

'Yes', I said. 'I mean, I don't have children or anything, but I have, you know, like brothers and a sister ...' God, I was rambling.

'Very wise', said Jean-Philippe. 'Myself, I don't want children. But you know it is difficult. My partner really wants children, but I don't.'

'Oh, that's tough. What will you do?'

'Well, I got a dog.' He shrugged. 'I got Douglas a dog.'

In my mind the bar suddenly went quiet. Please let me look normal, I thought, as the realisation hit me. Please let me be looking cool, like I knew. Oh my God, Jean-Philippe was on with Douglas. Jean-Philippe was still talking about something but I wasn't listening.

I looked over at Julie. She was talking to Douglas. They were both laughing. Julie was stroking his arm every time she leant forward and giggled. God, I thought, I have to let her know before she says or does something embarrassing—to them and us.

'Are you allowed to smoke in here?' I asked Jean-Philippe.

'Not until 9.30pm', he replied and said something about the horrors of not being able to smoke. I got up. 'I'm going outside to have a cigarette', I said. I shot Julie a look that screamed, come with me! She got up and walked over to where I was standing by the fire.

'I'll come too', said Douglas, getting up. Shit!

I grabbed Julie and quickly whispered in her ear, 'Jean-Philippe and Douglas are lovers'. She looked at me blankly. 'Jean-Philippe told me!' I added urgently.

'Right', said Julie, matter-of-factly.

The three of us walked outside. Julie, to her credit, was acting normal. I looked at Douglas. He was clearly enjoying our company. He hung on everything we said and genuinely seemed to be really into us. How could this be true?

For the rest of the night Jean-Philippe talked to the Flying Kangaroo and Douglas, Julie and I talked. And talked and talked and laughed and laughed. After a while the earlier revelation didn't seem to matter. We were having such a great time.

I told Julie and Douglas that in the morning I was interviewing Clio Cresswell, a mathematician who had written a book called *Mathematics and Sex*. According to her, sex and relationships are a matter of maths and good sex is a case of knowing the right equation. It started a riotous debate and a whole lot more laughter.

'I don't think that is right', insisted Douglas. 'I think there is something more than that. There's attraction. There's chemistry ...'

'I know', I agreed. 'You can tell even before you know someone if there is an attraction or chemistry. You can tell by looking in someone's eyes ...'

'Do you really believe that?' asked Douglas, with some urgency, and looking straight into my eyes. He touched my hand.

'Yes, I do', I said.

Douglas turned to Julie and me. 'My friend', he said, signalling to the Flying Kangaroo, 'asked me when you arrived how I knew you both, and I said they are students at the Alliance. And he said, but how can that be? Everyone at the Alliance is so dull and boring?' He paused. 'I told him that when you walk into the Alliance it is like a light comes shining through the door.'

Julie and I gasped. 'It's true', he said.

Over the next few hours the drinking and conversation flowed. Douglas walked Julie and me back to our car. It was still parked in the Alliance Française car park, which was now locked.

'When are you coming to Belgium?' asked Douglas, hugging us goodbye.

'We want to come at the beginning of next year', I said.

'Really?' stressed Douglas. 'You will come and you will stay with me in Ghent?'

We assured him that we would and with that he unlocked the gates and disappeared into the night.

Chapter 34
Next stop, Cannes

Verb drills: *aller* (to go)
L'Imparfait:
J'allais ... (I was going ...)   *nous allions* ... (We were going ...)

Le futur:
J'irai ... (I will go ...)   *nous irons* ... (We will go ...)

Le conditionnel:
J'irais ... (I would go ...)   *Nous irions* ... (We would go ...)

Julie and I were sitting around my kitchen table, which was covered with printed copies of entertainment articles we had written over the years.

'Okay, we have five articles that are about European films', I stated. Julie looked down at her list.

'Well, that's enough', she said, 'now we need four articles with your by-line and my by-line, signed by the authors'.

'Do you think they should be ones with a French leaning?'

'Not necessarily,' Julie said, thoughtfully, 'they should probably include a mixture of hard-hitting journalism, so we look like, you know, proper journalists, and also some with some big names, not necessarily of film. Here, we should definitely have this wrap-up that we did of the Academy Awards'.

After a couple of hours, and several coffees, we had our six piles of articles, all painstakingly selected. Julie was carefully labelling each pile with descriptions in French—so carefully that she was looking up even the most basic word in the dictionary.

'We just need to put in the letter of authority from the publishers and the covering letter. *Voilà.*'

We stood for a moment and regarded the pile of paper on the table. Our application for press accreditation at the Cannes Film Festival.

Well, actually it was our application to apply for an application to the film festival. I had contacted the press office at Cannes and they emailed me a very specific list of instructions. We must send the office a parcel of articles and permissions, all to their specific criteria. They would review them and then, if satisfied, would *invite* us to apply for accreditation.

'Press accreditations are as rare as titanium-plated hens' teeth', the instructions had read, and we could understand why. The Cannes Film Festival, held every year in the south of France, is undoubtedly the most glamorous event on the movie world calendar. It is a week filled with champagne, parties, designer frocks; all the huge names in film attend.

Later, when we had ceremoniously deposited the parcel in the mailbox, Julie showed me the plan of action she had drawn up. 'We'll leave at the end of April and spend a week in Ghent with Douglas, and then we'll go to Paris for a week. Margie, do you know that you can call stores in Paris and tell them you are going to Cannes, and they *lend* you designer dresses? And then we'll go to Cannes.'

It didn't really surprise me that Julie had scheduled a visit to see Douglas. After the Weekend *d'Amour*, Laurant had been an out-of-bounds topic, while discovering Douglas could never be hers had not dulled Julie's enthusiasm one bit. In fact, she was closer to him than ever. They emailed each other regularly and Julie even mailed him posters and books of Australian landscapes, which he adored.

'You know,' I observed, 'Australia is to Douglas what France is to us'.

Neither Julie nor I were disappointed that Douglas ended up being gay. Shocked, yes, but not upset. Okay, very shocked, it did take several weekends of talking it through before we were able to resolve ourselves to it, but the fact is our feelings for Douglas had changed. That night, Douglas went from being the object of Julie's infatuation to a dear friend. And neither of us could be disappointed with that.

One night, while we were re-enrolling for Conversation and Grammar classes, Julie asked Benjamin, 'Have you heard from Douglas since he's been back in Belgium?'

Benjamin scoffed, 'Douglas and I are different people. I am young and alive and he likes old people'.

Julie frowned. 'Well, at least Douglas isn't a *con* (dickhead).'

Benjamin was stunned, and even I was shocked at Julie's outburst. 'You can't say anything bad about my Douglas', she muttered as we left the building. In truth, the Douglas episode was a reflection of our whole experience of learning French. Not at all what we had anticipated, but special in its own way.

When Freda and I walked into the Alliance Française de Melbourne at the end of 1999, we anticipated spending Thursday evenings learning vocabulary surrounded by like-minded Francophiles and glamorous French teachers. We couldn't foresee the frustrations, humiliations and despair that come with learning another language. We couldn't have imagined the freaks with which we would be surrounding ourselves, the odd assortment of teachers and the politics and power struggles of the classroom. Yet, I also never anticipated meeting Julie, my best friend and the only person I know who had the same desire to become French as me.

Most surprising of all, I discovered a side of myself that I never knew I had. I never considered myself a 'language' person, like my sister, who seems to have no trouble picking up foreign languages. I know now that I have the strength to stick to a goal even in the face of humiliation, frustration and a whole lot of hard work. And I no longer feel as though I have to be in control of everything around me. I'm more comfortable than ever saying 'I don't understand' or 'I don't know', and I know the world doesn't come to an end when I do.

The editor of *The Connexion* was impressed with the two articles I wrote for her and was keen to commission more. I was still supplying articles to other English-language magazines in France.

In the months ahead a few French men crossed our paths. There was Pierre, the tall, dark guy who installed French satellite TV into our homes. Etienne, the older French native, who joined our French class essentially to make friends with Francophiles; and Robert, a young, funky French guy we met at The Lounge who decided to come up and introduce himself when he saw us doing our French homework. Yet, while there was a time when Julie just needed to know a guy was French before she could start her seduction routine, she didn't respond to any of them. In fact, as far as I could tell, she wasn't dating at all.

'I'm holding out for Cannes', she said, with a twinkle in her eyes. 'For when I get Daniel Auteuil.'